Shays's Rebellion

WITNESS TO HISTORY

Peter Charles Hoffer and Williamjames Hull Hoffer, *Series Editors*

# Shays's Rebellion

## Authority and Distress in Post-Revolutionary America

SEAN CONDON

Johns Hopkins University Press | *Baltimore*

© 2015 Johns Hopkins University Press
All rights reserved. Published 2015
Printed in the United States of America on acid-free paper
9 8 7 6 5 4 3 2 1

Johns Hopkins University Press
2715 North Charles Street
Baltimore, Maryland 21218-4363
www.press.jhu.edu

Library of Congress Cataloging-in-Publication Data

Condon, Sean, 1970–
    Shays's Rebellion : authority and distress in post-revolutionary America /
Sean Condon.
        pages cm — (Witness to history)
    Includes bibliographical references and index.
    ISBN 978-1-4214-1742-4 (hardcover : acid-free paper) — ISBN 978-
1-4214-1743-1 (paperback : acid-free paper) — ISBN 978-1-4214-1744-8
(electronic) — ISBN 1-4214-1742-1 (hardcover : acid-free paper) — ISBN
1-4214-1743-X (paperback : acid-free paper) — ISBN 1-4214-1744-8
(electronic) 1. Shays' Rebellion, 1786–1787. 2. Government, Resistance
to—Massachusetts—History—18th century. 3. Authority—Political aspects—
Massachusetts—History—18th century. 4. Massachusetts—Politics and
government—1775–1865. I. Title. II. Title: Shays' Rebellion.
    F69.C68 2015
    974.4'02—dc23    2014043197

A catalog record for this book is available from the British Library.

*Special discounts are available for bulk purchases of this book. For more
information, please contact Special Sales at 410-516-6936 or specialsales@press
.jhu.edu.*

Johns Hopkins University Press uses environmentally friendly book materials,
including recycled text paper that is composed of at least 30 percent post-
consumer waste, whenever possible.

974.4
CON

To Liz, with love

# Contents

Shays's Rebellion

# Worcester, Massachusetts, September 5–6, 1786

ON THE MORNING OF Tuesday, September 5, 1786, a crowd of approximately two hundred men marched through the streets of Worcester, Massachusetts, and headed for the courthouse. Some of the men marched with sticks or clubs, while others carried guns with bayonets fixed. Accompanied by fife and drum, the men paraded to the entrance of the courthouse, stopped, and waited. Later that morning, another procession made its way toward the courthouse, led by Worcester county sheriff William Greenleaf, followed by judges and a number of lawyers. These men were coming to open the scheduled session of the Court of Common Pleas, the lower court that met four times a year in each county of the Commonwealth of Massachusetts to handle civil cases like debt litigation. As the procession reached the courthouse, the crowd of men "opened to the right and left," but six armed members of the crowd remained guarding the courthouse door, with their guns raised, preventing the sheriff and judges from entering.[1]

One of the judges, Artemas Ward, approached the men and "demanded repeatedly who the Commanders of that party were, and by what authority they assembled in that hostile manner and why those bayonets were placed at his Breast."[2] Ward was well known to the people of Worcester County, and he was accustomed to commanding respect. A native of the town of Shrewsbury, he was a Harvard graduate, a prosperous farmer and merchant, and a veteran of both the French and Indian War and Revolutionary War. In fact, on the day after the battle of Lexington and Concord he had been named commander of the patriot armed forces that opposed the British in Boston, a position he held until the Continental Congress took charge of the army and named George Washington as his replacement. Ward had served for several years as a judge and as a member of the state legislature, even rising to serve as the speaker of that body.[3] But on this day in Worcester, none of the men blocking Ward budged but instead "remained firm and very insolent." Ward addressed the crowd, telling them that what they were doing "was rebellion against Government, and must be suppressed or Government would be at an end."[4] Ward's speech moved no one, and the judges were forced to retreat to a nearby tavern, where they ate a meal and agreed to try and reconvene the next morning.

While Ward did not recognize any of the leaders of the crowd blocking the courthouse, Sheriff Greenleaf and other observers did. In a letter to the governor following the incident, Greenleaf identified eleven men from five different nearby towns as the leaders.[5] While none of these men had attended Harvard or achieved the rank of general, many of them were veterans of the Revolutionary War. For example, one of the men, Adam Wheeler of Hubbardstown was among those who had responded to the alarm for Lexington and Concord, and he went on to serve for several more years as a captain in a number of other notable campaigns.[6]

Wheeler later wrote an open letter to explain his involvement in the crowd action at Worcester. Refuting General Ward, he said that he had "no intention to destroy the publick government." Instead, he had helped stop the court because he had been "moved with the distress of the people." He had seen too many "valuable and industrious members of society" who had gotten into debt or were behind on their taxes and, as a result, had been "dragged from their families to prison, to the great damage not only of their families but the community at large." Wheeler reminded his audience of his Revolutionary War service and said that he had "stepped forth in the defence of this country" in order to gain the "glorious prize" of liberty. He said that the crowd's action in Worcester was a continuation of that fight: "Liberty is the prize I still have in view, and in this glorious cause I am determined to stand with firmness and resolution."[7]

With the crowd in control of the courthouse, the sheriff and the court officers were visited by representatives of the crowd who presented them with a petition asking for a postponement of all cases in which debtors might lose property. In the midst of this activity, the court officers and the sheriff put out a call for militia forces to come to the defense of the court, so that it could proceed with its business. In fact, the court in neighboring Hampshire County had been closed by a crowd the week before, and Massachusetts governor James Bowdoin had already alerted Worcester County militia commander Jonathan Warner that the militia might be needed. In response, Warner had assured Bowdoin that he would pass the message down to his militia officers. But no local militia force arrived. The crowd remained in control of the courthouse and was joined the next day by more unarmed supporters.

As General Warner explained later, many were reluctant to take up arms in support of the government, "notwithstanding the most pressing orders for them to turn out & to appear at Worcester equipped as the law directs." According to Warner, some of the men had engaged in "evasion or delay," while others responded to the call with "a flat denial."[8] Some of the militia officers believed that the reason they were not able to raise a force to protect the court was that rank-and-file militia members were "too generally in favor of the people's measures."[9] As a result, Artemas Ward and the other judges were forced to accede to the crowd's demands and adjourn the court session on Wednesday, September 6. After the court agreed to an adjournment, part of the crowd paraded before the house in which the judges were staying. These two hundred or so men, "armed with sticks only," waited there for about an hour, and then the main force, which had stood by the courthouse, marched with their guns toward the others, who opened a path for them to walk through, and then the whole crowd proceeded to the town meeting house.[10]

As members of the crowd dispersed to return to their own homes, some of them may have remembered that exactly twelve years earlier, on September 6, 1774, another (significantly larger) Worcester crowd had closed the courts to protest the "Intolerable Acts" imposed by the British in response to the Boston Tea Party.[11] One act in particular, the Massachusetts Government Act, had authorized significant changes to the colony's 1691 charter that shifted authority from Massachusetts's towns and its assembly to the royal governor. The towns responded by organizing county conventions, where town representatives declared the new acts illegitimate because they violated the colony's charter. The county conventions also advocated direct crowd action, including intimidation of royal appointees and forced closure of the county courts. The closure of the Worcester County court had been one of the events that helped catapult the American colonies into a war for independence from Great Britain. Practically everyone living in Worcester in 1786 was proud of that revolution, and many had made significant sacrifices to help make independence a reality.

Now, however, a new conflict had emerged. What had led men like Adam Wheeler to confront their government with some of the same tactics that were used against the British, and how would authorities like Artemas Ward and Governor James Bowdoin respond? How would the conflict play itself out, and what impact would it have on the Commonwealth of Massachusetts and on the United States as a whole? To address these questions, the narrative begins in 1780, when colonists in Massachusetts were struggling to secure their independence and to fashion a legitimate government.

# *1* Paying for Independence

A CONVENTION IN Cambridge, Massachusetts, voted in March 1780 to approve a draft of the state constitution and send it to all of the state's towns for review and ratification. Ever since the military conflict with Great Britain had begun in 1775, the Massachusetts government had been operating under a modified version of its colonial charter. While many in the state had originally believed that this wartime arrangement would be suitable and legitimate for the duration of the war, others did not agree. The earliest and most sustained criticism emerged in far-western Berkshire County among a group of men upset that the state's governing council had taken over where the colonial governor had left off by continuing to appoint legal officials for counties without direct input from the people. As a 1775 petition from Pittsfield resident Thomas Allen put it, "If the right of nominating to office is not invested in the people we are indifferent who assumes it whether any particular persons on this or the other side of the water."[1] The petition went on to argue that the people of Massachusetts should take their time to frame a new government and that, in the meantime, local committees would preserve order and provide whatever was needed to win independence from Great Britain. In many parts of Massachusetts, the county courts had been closed to protest against the British, and in some counties they continued to remain so. Allen and his allies—who would become known as the Berkshire Constitutionalists—argued that the local courts should not reopen until a state constitution was crafted and ratified by the people.

Following the formal Declaration of Independence in July 1776—which established that legitimate governments protected people's rights and must have the "consent of the governed"—more and more people in Massachusetts agreed with the Berkshire Constitutionalists that a new framework of government was needed. In the fall of 1776, the state legislature asked for permission to craft a constitution, present it to the public for comment, and then vote on it. Most towns responded that a new constitution was needed but that the people themselves should ratify the document. In 1777 the legislature decided to craft a constitution and then send it to the towns for ratification, but for a variety of reasons this constitution of 1778 was overwhelmingly rejected by Massachusetts towns. The following year, the legislature agreed to call for a separate constitutional convention, which began meeting in the fall of 1779 to formulate a draft constitution. A principal architect of this constitution was John Adams, who believed that one of the primary challenges facing representative forms of government was their susceptibility to division and internal conflict. Adams believed that part of a solution to that problem was to recognize that there were inevitable distinctions between commoners and elites that needed to be maintained in the constitution. All citizens had the same basic rights and freedoms, but different classes of people had different interests, and a framework of government that balanced those competing interests would have, Adams believed, the best chance at stability and survival.[2]

The document that was eventually created was shaped by debate in committee and in the full convention, but it was built upon Adams's belief that power had to be balanced between the many and the few. The document called for a governor and a bicameral legislature with a House of Representatives—where representation would be based on a town's population—and a Senate, where people would be elected to represent counties. In some ways, the document encouraged broad participation by the electorate: elections would be held every year, and voters would directly elect both branches of the legislature as well as the governor and lieutenant governor. On the other hand, there was a property qualification of £60 in order to vote, and higher minimum property qualifications to serve in government: £200 to serve in the House, £300 to serve in the Senate, and £1,000 to serve as governor. In addition, the governor and his council would have the ability to name court justices without formal input from individual counties. During the ratifying convention, representatives from western towns fought to have travel expenses of legislators paid for by the state, and not by the individual towns, because they argued that many less wealthy and more distant towns could not afford to send a representative to be present for entire sessions, if at all. However, their efforts proved unsuccessful.[3]

In March 1780, copies of the draft constitution were printed in Boston and sent to each of the state's more than three hundred towns, collectively home to more than a quarter of a million people. The largest—with a population of more than 15,000—was the capital and port city of Boston. It and many of the surrounding communities had been settled by the English for a century and a half, and they included towns along the coast from Cape Cod to Maine, dominated by fishing and Atlantic trade, and inland towns of farmers, most of whom could trace their land holdings back for several generations. Further west, the terrain became more hilly and was composed of the farming communities of Worcester and Hampshire counties, thirty to sixty miles or more from the city of Boston. Most of these communities had begun as offshoots of eastern towns, and were generally smaller and less well-established versions of their eastern counterparts. Within Hampshire County, some settlements along the Connecticut River such as Springfield and Northampton had been in existence for more than century, and many of these Connecticut River valley settlements included merchants who made their living selling surplus farm products from interior towns to the Atlantic market, while providing their neighbors with manufactured goods and commodities originating from distant markets, especially tea, sugar, and rum. Beyond the Connecticut River valley lay the Berkshire Mountains, and some communities there and in Hampshire County were still in the process of being settled. These farthest communities were more than one hundred miles away from Boston, a trip that typically took several days on horseback if one had reason to go.

No matter what the town's size, location, or wealth, the male heads of each household would come together in regular town meetings to make collective decisions about who should be named constable, how much money should be paid to the town's congregational minister, and who would represent the town in the colonial legislature. In addition, able-bodied adult male town residents between the ages of sixteen and sixty were responsible for

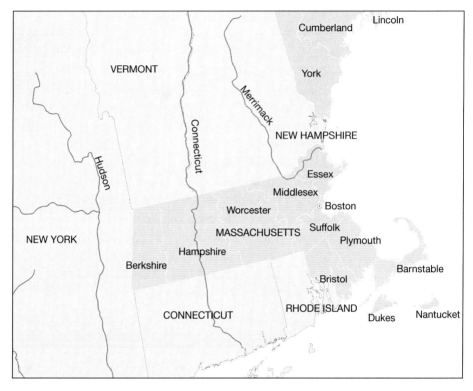

Massachusetts counties in the 1780s.

being available for militia service. These men would periodically train on the town common, and officers in the militia were selected by the militia members and tended to be more established men who were entrusted with other town responsibilities. The composition and organization of the militia in Massachusetts meant that members of each unit were well known to each other and typically bound by deep and intricate ties of kinship and neighborhood. Such men had been essential to forming and maintaining an armed revolutionary force, and in the spring of 1780 they were called together to assess the proposed constitution and determine whether their town supported or opposed the document.

According to the rules developed by the constitutional convention, towns were requested to vote separately on each article of the constitution, and each article that did not receive a two-thirds vote was to be revised by the convention.[4] Altogether, 290 towns responded, and only 42 of them voted to accept the constitution without amendment. Most towns examined each element of the document separately, and they often included their own commentary in their returns. For example, the town of Shelburne voted separately on all 124 paragraphs of the proposed constitution, approving some paragraphs unanimously and others by majority vote, while voting against 20 of the paragraphs. For every paragraph voted down, the town identified the reason or reasons for the negative vote. For example, its objection to what it called Article II, Section II, Paragraph One (which specified property qualifications for voters) stated: "Every man that is free . . . twenty one years of age and is liable to Taxation ought to give in his vote in all Political affairs."[5] Forty-one other towns, most of them in the western part of the state, joined Shelburne to object to the need for property qualifications to vote, while a few towns wanted to require higher qualifications for those serving in office. Other towns not only listed objections but also recommended specific changes or amendments to the proposed document.

To examine the returns, the convention formed a committee that began meeting on June 7, 1780. It found some objections to every article, with issues about voting and representation and the relationship between church and state proving to be the most contentious. However, as historians Samuel Eliot Morrison and Stephen Patterson have shown, the "revising and arranging" committee counted the returns in such a way as to emphasize support and deemphasize opposition. The committee decided that it would count the returns for each article of the constitution, but it would count the negative votes from a town only for each article that had a separate vote. For example, Northbridge voted 38-0 against the constitution without amendments, but the committee did not count any negative votes from Northbridge because the town did not vote separately on each article. Even if a town noted that it rejected a particular article but failed to record a vote, no negative votes would be recognized for that article. After a week of tallying the results, the committee determined that each article had received the two-thirds majority necessary. The following day, June 16, 1780, the convention agreed, and the Massachusetts Constitution was ratified.[6]

Elections were held for both houses of the legislature and for governor, and in October 1780 the new legislature gathered to hear an opening address from the newly elected governor John Hancock. Despite the irregular actions of the convention committee, most people in Massachusetts—including the Berkshire Constitutionalists—were ready to accept the new framework of government. By the time Massachusetts finally ratified its state constitution, it had been engaged in a war for independence for more than half a decade. In addition to the many sacrifices of military service and wartime deprivation, the state had experienced dramatic inflation brought on by increased wartime demand and the reliance of the Confederation Congress on paper currency to purchase supplies and pay troops. The runaway inflation that resulted caused considerable disruption and discord in Massachusetts and throughout the colonies. On the home front, while farmers who could produce surpluses could benefit from rising prices, they also had to pay much higher prices for consumer items like sugar, molasses, and rum. On several occasions, crowds confronted merchants who were accused of taking advantage of the wartime scarcity to gouge their customers, and in 1777 Massachusetts passed legislation that set price ceilings and empowered town communities and local officials to enforce such prices. Despite the new law, the price controls were not able to slow the pace of inflation in Massachusetts or other states, and the problem only got worse over the course of the summer of 1777, even with a revised price schedule in June of that year. By September, the Massachusetts legislature admitted that the plan had not worked, and the price control measure was repealed.[7] For their part, soldiers discovered to their dismay that inflation dramatically reduced the value of their pay until it was considered virtually worthless. Continental army soldier Joseph Plumb Martin remembered receiving $6.66 a month in such currency until the summer of 1777, "when paying ceased." He said that such pay was "scarcely enough to procure a man a dinner." After that, Martin noted, the money lost so much value that "Government was ashamed to tantalize the soldiers any longer with such trash," and it switched to offering soldiers certificates that promised interest and eventual payment of the face value of the certificate. Many, however, would be forced to exchange these certificates for far less than their face value.[8]

Following the ratification of the Massachusetts Constitution, the state legislature began to craft new fiscal and tax policies in order to combat the hyperinflation of the late 1770s and to assert authority over economic matters that had largely been in the hands of town committees (and occasionally crowds) in the early years of the war. The government in Boston endeavored to reduce the state's money supply and to rely instead on government-issued securities that promised annual interest payments and repayment of the face value of the security. In order to keep such promises, the state government

levied a series of direct taxes on the towns (in fact, as historians have calculated, the overall tax burden in the 1780s was several times higher than it had
been at the end of British imperial rule). These fiscal and tax policies were
championed by merchants and other commercially oriented citizens, but
they put significant pressure on many farming communities in the central
and western parts of the state. Many Massachusetts farmers carried personal
debt, and the 1780s brought high tax bills, a depressed economy, and creditors who were increasingly willing to sue to recover their debts. Early efforts
to reverse the course of the legislature's new fiscal and tax policies proved
unsuccessful, and as residents in the central and western part of the state
became increasingly convinced that government leaders in Boston were not
responsive to their needs, they began to organize and put pressure on local
authorities in ways that recalled protest against and resistance to the British.

## A Tender Conflict

The shift in state government policy began as an effort to rein in the hyperinflation of the late 1770s and to determine a new mechanism to finance
the war with Britain. In 1779 the Continental Congress had been forced to
recognize that its currency had lost nearly all of its value and that printing
any more currency would be useless. Instead, the congress asked states to call
in the old money and replace it with new currency. Massachusetts agreed by
calling in much of the continental currency in taxes in 1779 and then creating a new currency based on the old: for every forty dollars of paper money
already in circulation, the holder was entitled to two dollars of the new.[9] All
told, £460,000 worth of this new currency was printed. Earlier in the war,
the state government had attempted to stabilize the value of paper currency
by designating it "legal tender." In other words, sellers of goods and services
and creditors were required by law to accept this currency at face value. In
1779 the state government continued to use this strategy (by making the new
currency legal tender), but it also designated the new currency a government
security: the holders of the paper were entitled to 5 percent annual interest,
and a promise was made to pay the holders the principal in gold or silver coin
by the end of December 1788.[10]

Within a few months of the new currency emission, its value began to
decline. As they had done before, those who had something to sell responded
by either raising prices or withholding their goods and services from the

market. Creditors, however, did not have an immediate remedy, and they and their allies began to call for an end to the tender status of the new currency by arguing that it authorized a kind of legal theft: debtors were able to pay off their debts by exchanging paper that was worth considerably less than the value of what they had been loaned. One critic, writing in the *Massachusetts Spy* newspaper, argued that tender laws were "replete with more evils than were ever contained in Pandora's box" because they "obliged persons to receive certain sums of money of inferiour value to money lent or commodity sold."[11] On the other hand, those who wished to preserve the tender status of the new currency argued that ending it would harm debtors "(which are the poorer sort of the people)" and force them to "throw away their time and part of their own estates to keep good and make secure a part of the estates of their creditors (which are the richest of the community)." Supporters of tender status suspected that their opponents either were trying to stir up disunity or were selfish men interested in making "their own fortunes upon the ruin of the common people." From this perspective, creditors who wanted to get rid of tender status were hypocrites who hid their selfish motives "cloak'd under the specious pretext of honesty."[12]

By the early 1780s, personal debt had become a significant problem throughout Massachusetts. As had been the case in the colonial period, debtors could be sued by creditors to recover unpaid debts, and such debtors faced the prospect of having their property seized by a justice of the peace and sold at auction; or, if they claimed that they did not have sufficient property, debtors could be lodged in jail until they borrowed from someone else or otherwise came up with a way to pay off the debt. Most debts—especially those contracted among neighbors in farming communities—would likely never end up in court, but debt suits had been commonplace before the Revolutionary War. By all measures, however, the number of debt suits increased dramatically in the early 1780s.

In the fall of 1780, in the first session of the legislature following the ratification of the state constitution, critics of the tender status of the new currency pushed aggressively for repeal, but 63 percent of the state House of Representatives voted to maintain the tender status of the new currency. Despite this legislative defeat, the opponents of tender status redoubled their efforts at the next legislative session, which began in early January 1781. Advocates for repeal tended to draw their support from Boston and the more commercially oriented towns from the Atlantic Coast and the Connecticut

River valley, and their opponents were more likely to hail from more isolated interior towns where a debt suit might mean that a farmer would lose farm animals or other property that his family relied on for economic independence. Those residents of Massachusetts who were more commercially oriented necessarily operated in a broader Atlantic market, and therefore had to be concerned with what Massachusetts currency would be worth outside the state, whereas more isolated citizens of the commonwealth did not share such concerns. In between sessions, opponents of tender status continued to make arguments in state newspapers (which were heavily concentrated in Boston and other towns along the Atlantic coast), and they benefited when several dozen representatives from western towns failed to come to Boston for the January session of the legislature. Following a series of close votes, on January 25, 1781, the legislature repealed the tender status of the new currency, to the delight of creditors and to the dismay of many debtors and their allies. Instead of being accepted at face value, the new state currency would be periodically assessed by the state supreme court, which tied it more closely to its (declining) market value. As the currency's value declined, any debtors who used that currency to pay their creditors would need to use more to satisfy their debts.[13]

The primary reason why the tender status had been authorized in the first place was so that it might keep the value of the currency relatively stable. With the elimination of the tender provision, how could the currency's value be stabilized? Opponents of tender status argued that legal-tender currency should be replaced by (or converted into) government-issued securities that would be sought by private investors if they offered significant interest payments along with speedy repayment of principal at face value. The same legislative act of January 25, 1781, that changed the tender status also guaranteed the repayment of interest and principal—in gold and silver coin—by the end of 1786, which was two years earlier than promised in the previous law. Almost immediately, the January 25 law was attacked in many parts of the commonwealth, both because it threatened to impose greater burdens on private debtors and because it promised to enrich public creditors, that is, those men and women who held state securities. As early as February 1781, town representatives began to come together in county conventions in Suffolk, Middlesex, and Worcester counties to protest the new law. But while these county conventions did mobilize opposition, the new convention movement itself inspired considerable criticism. Back in 1774, such conven-

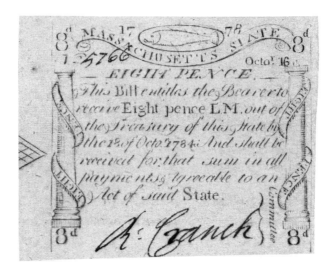

Front of eight-pence currency emitted by Massachusetts in 1778 to replace small-denomination currency originally printed in 1776 that had become "much torn and otherwise defaced" by 1778. This currency was deemed legal tender, and it states on the currency itself that it "shall be received for that sum [of eight pence] in all payments." One of the central challenges facing state and national governments during the Revolutionary War was paper currency's rapid loss of value. Early in the war, one method employed in an effort to limit currency devaluation was to deem currency legal tender, which meant that the currency could not be refused in exchange for goods or services or to pay off a debt. By the late 1770s and early 1780s, creditors and their allies in Massachusetts would fight successfully to end tender status for currency issued in the 1770s. For the legislation authorizing this currency emission, see *The Acts and Resolves . . . of the Province of the Massachusetts Bay . . .* (Boston, 1886), V:906–8. Source: Wikimedia Commons, http://commons.wikimedia.org/wiki/File:US-Colonial_(MA-258)-Massachusetts-16_Oct_1778_(OBV).jpg.

tions had played an important role in organizing against the British, but by 1781 many saw their continued existence as illegitimate. As one critic put it, such meetings were necessary and proper when the country was "without form and void, and darkness covered the face of our land." However, now that the state possessed a "new and regular constitution of government," any criticisms should be brought to the representatives, and debated by them in the legislature.[14]

Some feared that county conventions, in addition to being unconstitutional and improper, were more susceptible to local views that might be uninformed and potentially divisive. For example, when the town of Sutton in Worcester County proposed a county convention in the spring of 1781, one critic feared that persuasive convention representatives might pressure fellow representatives to accept dubious ideas, and as a result such conventions might end up with resolutions where "what is wanting in quality may be made up in quantity."[15] Another supporter of the tender law repeal (and critic of county conventions) echoed these concerns of local democracy run amuck. Calling himself "Sydney," he penned a defense of the tender repeal in the *Massachusetts Spy*. His support took the form of a fictional scene in a tavern, in which a farmer—who wanted paper money to be accepted as legal tender—discussed the issue with a schoolteacher, who believed that a legal tender law was not a good idea. In Sydney's scenario, the schoolteacher was able to change the farmer's mind by patiently explaining the ill effects of tender laws. Sydney's message was that opposition to the law was based on an uninformed and self-concerned electorate:

> One great misfortune is, that from the highest to the lowest we are accomplished statesmen, and in our little circles at the tavern, one likes this measure because our neighbor does, another disapproves of that because he is obliged to sell a sheep to pay his taxes; and in general you will find those who are grossly ignorant, who are not able to read one word in their Bible, much less write their own names, the most clamorous, and scrutinizing on the measures of government, than any other set of men.[16]

Despite—or perhaps because of—such condescending critiques, county conventions, towns, and individuals continued to attack the new law, which forced the Massachusetts legislature to respond in a formal "Address to the People." In this address from February 26, 1781, the legislature defended the law of January 25, noting that under the old tender act, a debtor could "deprive his creditor of seven fifteenths of his property, without remedy." This, according to the legislature, had to be ended as a matter of fairness and justice.[17] Many towns in the interior, however, did not agree, and in the annual spring elections they returned a majority of representatives who supported a return of tender status to the currency in a vote taken in June 1781. However, the state senate, which was much more sympathetic to the views of creditors, prevented passage of the bill.[18]

## State Taxation

Of course, as both supporters and opponents of the new fiscal laws recognized, the only way that the state government could credibly promise to offer regular and competitive interest and quickly repay the principal would be by raising considerably more revenue. The state would attempt to do so partly through impost and excise taxes on trade, but it would also have to implement significant direct taxation of the towns themselves. Along with interest on its own debt—and its operating expenses—the state had two other primary financial responsibilities. First, after 1779 the state was directly charged with providing troops and supplies for the state's share of the Continental army, or what was known as the "Massachusetts Line." Second, the state pledged to pay its share of the Continental debt. According to the Articles of Confederation—which had been drafted in 1777 and ratified in 1781—the national Congress had the authority to print and borrow money, but it did not have the power to directly tax the people of the United States. After the early strategy of relying on paper money began to break down, Congress borrowed from both foreign and domestic creditors. In order to pay off those debts, the central Congress determined how much money it needed to raise, and then it sent "requisitions" to the states, which were essentially requests to submit the necessary funds. Periodically, the federal government would send these requests to the states and leave it up to the states themselves to determine how each request would be met. For example, in 1782 the Congress determined that it needed $8 million from the states, and requisitioned nearly $1.3 million from Massachusetts, due in four quarterly payments. This requisition led to the passage of the state's first of two direct tax levies of 1782.[19]

From the perspective of many in the Massachusetts state legislature, these government debts should be paid off as quickly as possible. To do so, the Massachusetts legislature authorized nine separate direct taxes between 1780 and 1786.[20] The taxes in the 1770s were to be paid in Continental currency (in order to try and reduce the amount of currency in circulation) or beef. The two taxes in 1781 were due in gold or silver coin (also known as specie), while later state taxes would be due in beef, specie, or different government bills. No matter what kind of payment was required, direct state taxes were collected in the same way throughout the 1780s. Once the total amount of tax was determined by the legislature, a legislative committee determined each town's share, and the legislature authorized the state treasurer to issue a warrant to each town. For example, in 1781 the legislature authorized two taxes. The first, passed in May, levied more than £374,000 in taxes, more than half of which was to go to bounties for troops raised in 1780. For that tax, the town of Boston was responsible for more than £15,500, whereas the town of Worcester's share was roughly one-ninth that of Boston's. In far-western Berkshire County, in the recently settled town of Washington, the town was assessed a total of £254.

Whatever the town's size, the process of collection was the same: a warrant from the state treasurer was sent to the town assessor or assessors, whose job it was to determine what each household would have to pay. Most of the state's direct taxes consisted of a "poll" tax (a fixed amount levied on each able-bodied man aged seventeen or older), a property tax, and—if one were engaged in a profession (e.g., a blacksmith or lawyer)—an income tax. It was the assessor's job to determine how much tax was owed by each household, the amount based on the number of "polls," the amount of property, and the amount of income. Assessors made an announcement in town meetings or otherwise directed the people of the town to bring "true and perfect Lists of their Polls and of all Real and Personal Estate they are possessed of." Assessors had the authority to reduce or eliminate entirely the tax responsibility of any member of the town that they judged to be unable to pay through "Age, Infirmity or Poverty."[21]

Once they had determined the tax bill for each household in their town, the assessors turned over their lists to another locally elected official, the constable or collector of the tax. For the tax passed in mid-May 1781, the assessor was supposed to complete his work by the last day in June of that year, and collectors were charged with turning in tax payments by the end of August. If someone refused to pay their tax, collectors had the authority to seize property and auction it off in order to satisfy the tax bill. While the collector had considerable authority, he was also liable if he failed to complete his work. If collectors were late in submitting their taxes, or if they submitted less than the full amount, the state treasurer would inform the sheriff in the collector's home county, and the sheriff had the authority to seize the collector's property or lodge the collector himself in jail.[22] However, for much of the 1780s sheriffs were able to use their discretion, and if they believed that the collectors were not at fault, they would return the treasurer's execution without taking action against the collector.[23] Sheriffs in many parts of the state, especially in the western counties of Berkshire, Hampshire, and

Worcester, as well as the counties in Maine, were reluctant to put that kind of pressure on the collector. However, it was always within their authority to do so.

Collecting the tax in Massachusetts was therefore a challenge, because it put the tax collector himself at risk. If he pressed hard to collect, or seemed unreasonable, there was a risk of alienating neighbors and friends. If, on the other hand, he avoided confrontations with taxpayers, the tax collector put his own property (and liberty) in jeopardy. Because of their intimate interaction with their neighbors, and because their fates were tied to the people from whom they collected, some collectors became spokesmen for tax relief. For example, those charged with collecting the 1781 taxes in the town of Berwick (in the district of Maine) petitioned the legislature in May 1783 on behalf of the delinquent taxpayers in their town. They mentioned that part of the problem was that farmers in the town had been struggling with drought, which had made their farms less productive. But according to the Berwick collectors, the big challenge in collecting taxes was the large number of poor people in the town. They said they were unable to collect taxes from these townspeople "unless we are put to the disagreeable necessity to take from them their Cows which is all they have to support themselves and Families." Because of the hardship such taxation would impose, the Berwick collectors petitioned for a delay in collection and promised to "continue to use the best of our Endeavours to collect the Taxes and pay them in as soon as possible."[24]

While those in Berwick petitioned for relief, most town collectors did what they could to collect the taxes due. In the town of Lanesborough, in far-western Berkshire County, the man responsible for the tax collection in 1782 was Constable Ebenezer Buck. In April, Buck was attempting to finish collecting the October 1781 specie tax, in which the legislature had determined that Lanesborough owed £1,272.[25] According to the letter of the law, the deadline for submitting the returns was April 15. Early that month, Buck visited the home of town resident Perez Dean, who had apparently rebuffed an earlier visit from Buck. On this day Buck presented Dean with an order to seize Dean's cow, sell it, and apply the proceeds toward Dean's tax bill. Buck asked a passerby to help him collect the animal and "secure said cow for public auction." As Buck prepared to lead the cow away, Dean became extremely upset, and he called to one of his sons to fetch their neighbor, Justice of the Peace James Harris. Harris had been part of a Berkshire County committee that advocated tax relief, and when he emerged from his house and discovered what was happening, he told Buck that he would not allow him to take away his neighbor's cow. He said that it was not the first time that neighborhood livestock had been seized for taxes, and he threatened Buck by telling him that "we have got Men or could raise Men enough" to prevent any further seizures from taking place. In the meantime, Dean took advantage of Harris's appearance to lead his cow away from the constable, while Harris pressed his critique: he said it was "a shameful thing to take off a Cow for one dollar, and it should not be done." According to Harris, anyone who engaged in such action "ought to have their asses kicked."[26]

Realizing that he had lost the chance to seize Dean's cow, Constable Buck responded by reminding Harris that he himself still owed taxes, and Buck had a warrant to seize Harris if he refused to pay. At first, Buck and Harris started walking to the meetinghouse in town, with the idea that Harris could borrow the money from a neighbor to pay his tax. After a fruitless visit to a neighbor's house, Harris refused to continue on. With the help of a passerby, Buck tried to seize Harris, but he "lay'd down and we could not get him up or make him go on towards town."[27] At this point, Harris's son arrived to help his father. The constable was forced to give up when Harris's son threatened him and began "menacing him with doubled fists."[28]

Constable Buck let Harris return home, but he did not give up trying to collect the taxes he owed. A short time later, Buck and Harris both attended the Lanesborough town meeting. At the meeting, Buck asked another inhabitant of the town, a man named Chaney Ensign, to help him seize Harris for nonpayment of taxes. Harris "then made an open declaration in said Meeting" and asked members of the town to prevent him from being seized. He told the assembled meeting "of the abuse he had received from Mr. Buck," but when some members of the meeting told him to pay his tax, Harris replied that "he had not money with him."[29] Harris then left the meeting, and Buck turned to follow. One member of the meeting, Ebenezer Squire, advised Buck not to use force to seize Harris, because he was worried that there might be "contrary minds" that could rush to aid Harris. Buck brushed Squire off, telling him that "Harris had used him so, that he was determined to keep him until he paid his rate."[30] Buck followed after Harris, caught up to him, and again began to demand Harris's tax payment. When Harris refused, Buck "pull[ed] a cane from Esq. Harrises hand with force." Harris responded by exclaiming "Goddam you you Son of a Bitch let me alone," and "& a scuffle ensued."[31] Harris then appealed to the assembled crowd, telling them that people's property should not be seized for taxes. On this day, no one was willing to come to Harris's aid, and one witness, identified as a "gentleman," stated that "I fully believe that the town of Lanesborough . . . approved of said Constable's conduct & I can say that said town have always cheerfully supported said constable in the Collection of Taxes." Realizing that he could not prevail, Harris then asked two members of the crowd if he could borrow money to pay his tax. No one obliged, and Harris was then taken into custody and brought to the home of Colonel Jonathan Allen, where he was to be held until he paid his taxes. By ten o'clock the next morning, Harris had been able to secure a loan, pay his tax, and be released.[32]

As this conflict between Harris and Buck suggests, the collection of taxes could be contentious, and tax collectors needed at least the tacit support of other members of the community, while those who wished to resist paying their taxes also needed the help of family, friends, and neighbors for their resistance to be successful. It is clear that the drama of tax collection could be played out in the homes, fields, and streets of communities throughout the commonwealth. Given the potential for conflict, tax collectors might return assessments to the treasurer without the full amount, especially if they believed that their county's sheriff would not enforce the letter of the law. In other cases, towns responded to this potential disruption by coming together in formal town meetings to request tax relief from the state legislature.

Petitions began in 1778, where at least seven towns requested tax relief, and the number of petitions increased every year through 1782. Most of the early petitions came from towns in the eastern third of the state, especially along the Atlantic Coast, where the British navy remained a threat until the end of the Revolutionary War. For example, in June 1778 the town of Wellfleet on Cape Cod petitioned for a reduction in the state tax of that year because so many people were engaged in the war efforts: "Great numbers of its inhabitants had removed out of town, and that the circumstances of such as remained were those of distress."[33] In 1779, twenty-three towns petitioned for relief, followed by twenty-seven more in 1780. The number ballooned to forty-one in 1781 and increased again to forty-six the following year.[34]

Over time, a greater share of tax relief petitions came from more isolated and poorer settlements in central and western Massachusetts. For example, Mount Washington in southwestern Berkshire County petitioned for tax relief in 1782. In its petition, the town told the legislature that it was located on a mountain and that to travel to the town from the "surrounding valleys is at all times difficult & at many times impossible." This isolation made selling any farm products very difficult and expensive. As a result, even when the people of the town made the challenging trek to sell their goods, "very frequently the money received thereby is not a resonable compensation for the Labour bestowed merely in the sale." The petitioners estimated that "the Taxes . . . the last twelve months is more than the full improved Value of all the property of the Said Town." If some relief was not granted, the people of Mount Washington believed that "the present proportion of taxation will reduce the said Town to desperation & ruin."[35]

While few towns were as isolated as Mount Washington, many faced similar difficulties: their distance from markets made selling farm surpluses difficult, time-consuming, and barely worth the trouble. And unlike earlier in the Revolutionary War, when nearby armies were looking to purchase farm products like wheat and beef, the market for such local farm goods had declined, along with prices. As prices fell, even communities that were better established and prosperous had difficulty paying their taxes. Despite the efforts of tax collectors in every community in the state, none of the taxes levied in the 1780s were fully collected. For example, in 1783 the state treasurer published the number of towns that were delinquent in paying the beef taxes levied in 1780 and 1781. In all, 199 towns, or nearly two-thirds of all the towns in the state, still owed at least some of these taxes. Of these towns, 92 were located in the three western counties of Worcester, Hampshire, and Berkshire, and 11 of the 12 towns in Bristol County were also delinquent.[36]

After the legislature refused to return paper money to legal tender and instead pressed forward with significant direct taxes, many communities elected representatives that advocated for different relief measures. In the fall of 1781, a bill was introduced that would have given judges discretion to allow debtors more time to pay their debts, while another proposal would have given debtors the right to have their property assessed by town officials, who would assign a value presumably higher than what such goods would fetch at auction. However, all of these measures failed to pass the legislature, which sparked a new round of county conventions in Hampshire, Berkshire, and Worcester counties.[37] These conventions again pressed for debt and tax relief, and the Hampshire County convention held in the town of Hadley on February 11, 1782, stated that as long as taxes were so high, debt suits should be suspended.[38] In April a Worcester County convention representing twenty-six different towns bemoaned the high rate of taxation and believed that such high taxes were not a necessity: "That it is the unanimous opinion of this Convention, that great part of the uneasiness now subsisting among the inhabitants of this County, is owing, in great measure, to their not having been satisfied in what manner, the IMMENSE SUMS of PUBLICK MONEY, which have for several years past, been assessed upon them, has been DISPOSED OF."[39] In Berkshire County, a crowd of three hundred did gather in late February to halt the court session in Pittsfield, but the crowd was met by another in support of the court. A petition was presented asking the judges to suspend debt cases until the next term of the court, but the judges refused.

By the spring of 1782, many in Massachusetts faced the twin threats of high taxes and significant personal debt. Failure to pay could mean either the loss of significant property or even a trip to jail. After efforts to redirect government tax and fiscal policy proved unsuccessful, a new series of conventions drew disdain and even some mockery. As historians have calculated, the epicenter of personal indebtedness was in Worcester County, but in the spring of 1782 armed protest against the government erupted not there but in Worcester's neighbor to the west, Hampshire County. Before the American Revolution, authority in Hampshire County had been dominated by a few wealthy Connecticut River valley merchant families (known collectively as the "River Gods"). The revolution shattered the River Gods' authority, and no new group of county leaders was able to secure the acceptance of county residents as a whole. By contrast, in neighboring Worcester County, more popular leaders who had experience of countywide political leadership in the colonial period had remained legitimate authority figures in the 1780s. Such Worcester authorities disliked the new fiscal and tax policies of the state legislature, but they advocated a convention movement that could mobilize support for fiscal reform. In Hampshire County, on the other hand, county conventions betrayed a lack of trust in local officials who had the authority to execute tax and fiscal policy by calling for more local control of such officials. In addition, some in Hampshire County wanted their conventions in 1782 to call for extralegal actions to forcibly close the county courts.[40]

## Samuel Ely's Constitution

On Saturday, January 5, 1782, a crowd gathered on the common in Sunderland, Massachusetts, a town north of Springfield on the Connecticut River in Hampshire County. The people were drawn by the passionate words of forty-one-year-old Samuel Ely, a Yale-educated former minister from the nearby town of Conway. Ely told the crowd that he believed that the state government was corrupt and that the new state constitution was deeply flawed. Government officials were paid too much, and they had too much power. As a result, Ely believed that none of them deserved the respect of the people and urged his audience to "pay no more regard to them than to puppies." He told the crowd that he had a better version of a constitution in his own pocket, one that "the Angel Gabriel could not find fault with." Ely did not share this new framework of government with his audience, but he encouraged those assembled to organize a convention that would call for a closure of the county courts. He had already visited many other Hampshire County towns, and he assured the crowd in Sunderland that there was deep support for decisive action. To send a message to government officials, Ely advocated not just closing the courts but also targeting local authorities: "Attornies, Sheriffs, and all officers should be sacrificed," including prominent lawyer John Chester Williams, whose "body should be given to the fowls of the air and the beasts of the field."[41]

On that winter Saturday in Sunderland, Ely was unable to convince the townspeople to call for a county convention, but over the next several weeks he visited many other towns in Hampshire County, spreading his gospel of resistance. In early February, he was arrested on charges of "treasonable practices" and questioned by Justice of the Peace Joseph Hawley, but he was eventually released. Undeterred by this personal encounter with law enforcement, Ely continued to advocate active confrontation with government, and by early April he was able to convince some county residents to gather when the county court met at Northampton. Witnesses heard Ely encourage the men in the crowd to arm themselves and attack the officers of the court: "Come on my brave boys, we will go to the wood pile and get clubs enough, and knock their grey wigs off, and send them out of the world in an instant." He was able to coax a group of men to go to the courthouse, but as it approached, many in the crowd began to think twice about what Ely was asking them to do. Although he continued to call for action, no one was ready to join him in an attack on the judges of the court. Perhaps sensing the mood of the crowd, court officials called for Ely's arrest, and county Sheriff Elisha Porter took Ely into custody. After being arraigned, Ely was granted bail until the Supreme Judicial Court session scheduled for Northampton at the end of April.[42]

When the court session opened on Tuesday, April 30, a crowd again gathered. This time, the people presented the court with a list of grievances. The judges read the grievances but told those assembled that the people should seek relief from the state legislature, not the courts. Though the crowd did not disperse, it allowed the court to convene. The next day, Samuel Ely was scheduled to turn himself in for his trial, and some authorities were concerned that there would be an attempt to rescue him. County Sheriff Elisha Porter then made a call for support, and "in a few minutes 300 persons and upwards appeared to the assistance of the sheriff."[43] Ely was taken off to jail and that Friday was brought before the judges. At first, he pleaded not guilty to sedition and other related charges, and his trial was slated for the following Monday. Over the weekend, authorities in Northampton heard that approximately two hundred men were gathering in an attempt to free Ely, so the sheriff called out the local militia, and the quick response again prevented any effort to disrupt the court. On Monday, Ely's trial took place as scheduled, and now he changed his plea to guilty and threw himself on the mercy of the court. Ely was required to post a two-hundred-pound bond promising three years of good behavior, and he received a fifty-pound fine and a six-month jail term. After the trial, Ely was delivered from Northampton to the jail in Springfield to serve his sentence.[44]

Several weeks later, on the morning of Wednesday, June 12, 1782, more than one hundred men "armed with swords, guns and bayonets" marched through Northampton on their way toward the Springfield jail where Ely was held.[45] According to a supporter of the government, the men acted like a military company on the march, as they "behaved with great Steadyness and good order and made no Stop in the Town." The people in Northampton raised an alarm, and about fifty men hastily assembled to begin the fifteen-mile trek along the Connecticut River toward Springfield. But they were not quick enough to prevent the men from reaching the jail unmolested. The men encountered few people when they arrived in Springfield, because many residents had traveled to the nearby town of Longmeadow to attend the funeral of the minister there. The armed men marched to the jailhouse, where they demanded the keys from the jailer. When he refused, the men "procured axes and levers" and set Ely free, along with his two cellmates: a man imprisoned for debt, and a runaway slave.[46]

After the daring prison break, Samuel Ely and his rescuers headed north, where they were pursued by supporters of government, including Hampshire

County sheriff Elisha Porter. At one point, a group of government supporters ran into Ely's rescuers near the town of South Hadley, and although both sides were armed, neither side fired its weapons, but a brawl erupted that lasted for the better part of fifteen minutes.[47] Later that day, a government force led by Sheriff Porter maneuvered between the insurgent men on horseback and those on foot. Another scuffle ensued, which gave Ely a chance to make his second escape in as many days. The two groups then agreed to talk, with each side choosing five representatives, and as a heavy rain began to fall, the men decided to go to the nearby town of Northampton to continue the negotiations. After several hours, the two sides agreed that the supporters of Ely would hand over three prisoners who would be held until Ely was found and brought back to jail, and the rest of the crowd would disperse. In exchange, Sheriff Porter and the other government supporters agreed to cosponsor a petition asking the state legislature to consider the grievances voiced by a recent Hampshire County convention "& grant such redress as they think most expedient for the Publick Benefit."[48]

Both sides probably expected that Ely would quickly be found, and certainly the three men held as prisoners hoped that their stay in the Northampton jail would be brief. However, two days passed without any sign of Ely. Meanwhile, a crowd again formed and made its way to Northampton to press for the release of the three prisoners. It demanded that Sheriff Porter release the three men, who would promise to return if Ely could not be found. Porter refused and told the people that they could either bring in Ely or petition the legislature for relief. Porter gave representatives of the crowd a note from the three hostages asking them to find and deliver Ely over. The crowd's representatives left, and Porter was hopeful that Ely would be quickly found and returned. But at midnight Porter began receiving information that the crowd was again "on the March with Fire Arms & swear that if opposition is made to them they will lay the town in Ashes."[49] The alarm was sounded in Northampton, and Porter sent word to neighboring towns to send support.

The next day, insurgents continued to assemble in Hatfield, near Northampton, and they took several government supporters hostage. The insurgents, whom Porter described as being "in the greatest rage imaginable," sent another committee to meet with Sheriff Porter. According to Porter, the representatives told him that if their demands were not met, the people of Northampton "should sleep in Hutts that night." Porter responded to this threat by telling the men that "if the Inhabitants of Northampton must sleep in Hutts—they must expect to sleep in their graves."[50] Porter gave the representatives notes from the prisoners begging them to disperse and find Ely. Perhaps believing that they were forgeries, the crowd's representatives ripped up the letters and went back to the crowd. The crowd then marched on the Northampton jail, where it was met by a force of government supporters. Another discussion began, and Sheriff Porter brought the crowd's representative, Captain Rueben Dickinson, to visit the prisoners in the jail. When Dickinson learned that the prisoners supported the return of Ely, he and the others said that they had been deceived "by some who wished for mischief." The insurgents retreated but remained in the area.

Back in Boston, Governor Hancock learned of the crisis, and he directed that the three prisoners be brought to Boston where they could be detained more securely, but his warrant arrived too late. Sheriff Porter had met with local justices of the peace, and they encouraged him to release the three men if they agreed to help secure Ely or turn themselves in if requested by the state legislature. Porter did so, and the release of the three men ended the crisis. In a letter sent to the governor immediately following the affair, Sheriff Porter explained that the justices of the peace whom he had consulted had recommended that the hostages be released because they were convinced of "the Impossibility of preventing Bloodshed if the two Parties met again." In addition, the crowd of people who demanded the release of the prisoners did not comprise irresponsible rebels but included, in the words of Sheriff Porter, "a number of (otherwise) truly respectable People."[51] Following this remarkable series of events, Ely would escape Hampshire County and make his way into Vermont. Within a short time, he began publicly criticizing the government in Vermont for the price of land, and he called government officials in Vermont a "pack of Villains" who should be overthrown.[52] Arrested in September, Ely was convicted of defamation and forced to leave the state. On his return to Massachusetts, he was arrested and brought to jail, but within several months and after several petitions, he was able to effect his release.[53]

## The Aftermath of Ely's Rebellion

Following Ely's escape into Vermont and subsequent arrest, the immediate crisis in Hampshire County was over, but it was unclear how the Massachusetts government should respond. Joseph Hawley, a resident of Northampton and a prominent figure in the independence movement, wrote to Northampton's legislative representative to make sure that state authorities were aware that the distress in the countryside was genuine and, if left unaddressed, could lead to widespread revolt. For Hawley, perhaps the biggest problem was the fact that Revolutionary War soldiers had been paid with government certificates and paper money. The paper was nearly worthless, and while the certificates might be worth something in the future, they could not be used to pay the taxes now due, unless they were sold at a deep discount. In fact, that is what many veterans had to do: they had "been obliged to put off" their certificates "to Sharpers." For these veterans, it became most frustrating when their taxes were due: "When their Collector is at their doors demanding the hard cash, they immediately burst out in rage and become desperate." Despite their anger and desperation, Hawley argued that most of the men he described had come to the defense of the court when Ely and his supporters had tried to shut it down. But Hawley warned that if something was not done soon to alleviate their distress, the former soldiers would join the mob: "They will become outrageous and the Numbers who will side with them will be irresistible." If that happened, it would become a dangerous and unpredictable situation: "Your Sheriffs and their herds of deputies will be like Stubble before devouring fire."[54]

Hawley identified not only the problems facing many veterans of the war but also the costs of the legal system as another area of great concern. A large percentage of debt cases entered the legal system because they were instigated by creditors who wanted to establish legal claim to a debtor's property in case that debtor had other debts or obligations, not because creditors and debtors disputed the terms of the debt. In such cases, debtors would not contest the suit but would still be liable for the court fees, and these fees were the same whether the debt was five shillings or five hundred pounds. In some cases, debtors owed nearly as much in fees as they did for the debt itself. Hawley and others argued that there should be a way for debtors to acknowledge the debt without having to pay such high fees. For example, back in 1776, the Massachusetts legislature had passed a "Confession" bill that had allowed debtors to acknowledge their debt without the high fees, but this law had been repealed the following year by legislators (some of whom happened to be lawyers themselves).

Hawley worried that if the legislature did not provide some relief, the internal conflict might doom the effort to secure independence. Hawley believed that if men like Samuel Ely could maintain a persistent presence, it might allow the British to reestablish control in New England: "If (as the Tories See clearly) such Insurgents prevail, Britain prevails."[55] Hawley argued that the legislature needed to send representatives out to the western third of the state in order to meet with the disaffected to better understand their problems and to more clearly articulate the reasons why the state legislature had authorized new taxes. Hawley added that those representatives needed to be "Sensible, honest, cool, and Patient."[56] He believed that many in the countryside felt like they had been betrayed by Revolutionary leaders back east. They doubted that the higher taxes were going to support the troops, but instead were enriching government authorities in Boston: "Many of the Insurgents say that our Soldiers get none of it—that it cost them Much to maintain the *Great Men* under George the 3rd, But vastly more under the Commonwealth and Congress."[57]

As the events unfolded in Hampshire County, the legislature met in Boston in an effort to respond. First, in order to give the state a greater ability to prevent additional uprisings, it suspended the writ of habeas corpus for six months.[58] This gave sheriffs the ability to arrest and detain anyone that they believed was a threat to public order. The legislature balanced this enlargement of law enforcement powers with some minor reforms intended to help debtors. It temporarily lowered the legal fees for most court actions in the civil courts, and it passed a law that gave debtors the ability to have their property appraised by three disinterested townspeople, and if the creditor demanded payment, they would have to accept the goods for the value determined by the assessors, making it likely that the debtor would lose less property than if the goods were sold at auction. These reforms did offer debtors some relief, but they were very limited. Creditors who did not want to be compelled to accept the property of debtors could wait the twelve months for the law to lapse before seeking payment. And the same legislation that lowered some court fees also raised many others.[59]

The legislature took two additional steps that helped to diminish hostility in the countryside, and the first dealt with taxation. Recognizing that tax collection was causing distress, they reduced the tax burden of several towns that had asked for relief and relaxed enforcement of tax collection by directing the treasurer to delay sending executions to delinquent tax collectors for taxes that were already outstanding. While there had been calls for a new direct tax, the legislature also decided that no new direct taxes would be levied that session.[60] The final legislative measure was a decision to send a legislative committee to meet directly with the disaffected so that they could better understand the local concerns and also explain more clearly the actions taken by the legislature. The three-man committee was selected on July 5, and it was composed of very prominent figures: Samuel Adams, General Artemas Ward, and Speaker of the House Nathaniel Gorham.[61] The three men left Boston and traveled to Hampshire County, with a goal of visiting each town in the county "where Discontent had in any great Degree Prevailed."[62] They traveled first to Conway and asked the inhabitants if they would identify a list of grievances. In response, the inhabitants held a formal town meeting in which they decided that their grievances could not be separated from the grievances of the county as whole. After the meeting ended, it was decided that a county convention should be held. The convention began meeting at Hatfield on August 7, and for four days the three members of the legislature met with representatives from more than forty of the towns in Hampshire County.

The result of the Hatfield convention was a petition to the legislature that included reassurances of local support for state government combined with calls for reform. The petitioners promised that they were loyal citizens who would make every effort to pay "all reasonable taxes as fast as they shall be able."[63] The petition asked that a pardon be given to all of those who took part in the disturbances (except for Samuel Ely himself) and that the writ of habeas corpus be restored. The petition also voiced concern over the high cost of government (including the salaries of public officials) and the courts. They asked for reforms that would lower the cost of the legal system, arguing that taxes for many communities were unsustainably high because lawmakers did not understand that, if "the distance of the County from market" was long, it was very difficult if not impossible for such people to raise the necessary revenue to pay their taxes.[64]

Adams, Ward, and Gorham returned to Boston certain that their visit had been successful. They had been able to listen directly to the grievances of many towns and at the same time explain why the legislature had adopted its current course. In his report on behalf of the committee, Samuel Adams assured the legislature that the men had been treated "with great Candor and respect." He was confident that "ungrounded Suggestions that had been insinuated into the minds of many honest Citizens have been removed."[65] Adams's comment suggested that—in his mind at least—the disturbances were as much the result of willful misinformation and disruptive rumors as they were signs of genuine distress in the countryside. Many in the state legislature, especially those from Boston and other commercially oriented towns, shared Adams's vision. So, while the mild reforms and the work of the three-man committee did serve to calm at least some of the anger and despair in the countryside, it did not fundamentally alter the economic circumstances. Taxes would remain high, property seizure for debt and failure to pay taxes would continue to be a very real threat for many, and legal fees would remain at relatively high levels.

As a result, for the next couple of years many in the Massachusetts countryside tried a variety of responses. Towns continued to make cases for direct relief for particular taxes, and county conventions occasionally met to press for legislative reforms. Isolated instances of direct resistance to the seizure and sale of property from delinquent debtors and taxpayers also took place. For example, at the same time that the Samuel Adams was visiting Hampshire County towns, there was an effort to halt a sheriff's sale in the town of Taunton in Plymouth County. Two oxen had been seized for unpaid taxes, but a group of men came to the sale in an effort to intimidate any possible bidders and compel a postponement of the auction. Several days later, the sheriff tried again, and this time friends of the delinquent taxpayer were opposed by several men determined to see the auction take place to ensure that the laws would be enforced. A fight broke out as men attempted to prevent bids, but the oxen were sold. The man with the winning bid then offered the owner a chance to pay his taxes and have his oxen returned, as he wanted only to show the assembled crowd that the laws must be followed.[66]

Another incident occurred in the fall of 1782, in the Berkshire County town of Adams, when a constable was attacked while trying to seize the livestock of a delinquent taxpayer. The men responsible were caught, pleaded guilty, and were required to pay a fine.[67] In another episode, a sheriff's deputy had seized a pair of oxen from a debtor, but several of the debtor's friends had taken the oxen back. The sheriff, Caleb Hyde, told Governor Hancock that there "was reason to suppose a combination against the collection of Debt." In other words, he believed that people were organizing resistance to debt collection. So Hyde organized a force of sixty men and went in pursuit of the men who attacked his deputy. His party encountered a group of men, and a fight ensued: "Blows and wounds were given and received on both sides." Hyde was able to arrest twenty-one men, and in the course of questioning Hyde discovered that an effort to organize resistance to the seizure of property had taken place.[68] This incident and others persuaded the legislature in February 1783 to maintain the suspension of habeas corpus for another four months.[69]

## Commutation

By the fall of 1782, distress was not just evident among the civilian population but was also becoming more apparent among those still serving in the Continental army. In the last week of December 1782, several officers traveled from the army encampment in Newburgh, New York, on the Hudson River to bring a petition to the Confederation Congress in session in Philadelphia. The petition had been drafted by General Henry Knox, who had the support of then Secretary of War Benjamin Lincoln.[70] The officers were upset because they felt that they had been treated unfairly: the pay they had received had depreciated in value, but in many cases they had been forced to exchange this paper in order "to prevent their families from actually starving." They felt that others were benefiting from their distress: "We complain that shadows have been offered to us while the substance has been gleaned by others."[71] The officers complained not only about their pay but that their allowances for food and clothing were far below what they had been promised when they enlisted. Back in 1780, Congress had promised officers a pension of half pay for life following the end of the war. Little of substance had been done since then, and the officers were concerned that this pension would not be funded by a Congress that had no money. The officer's petition offered to give up, or commute, that pension in exchange for five years of full pay following the end of the war. They warned Congress that they had "borne all that men can bear," and that the soldiers would not stand idly by: "Any further experiments on their patience may have fatal effects."[72]

These protestors found some willing allies in Philadelphia, like Superintendent of Finance Robert Morris, who wanted the national government to have the authority to raise revenue directly instead of requisitioning the states. Morris and his allies encouraged dissent among the officers so that pressure would be put on Congress to seek greater authority to collect revenue, and the disaffected officers told Congress that unless something was done, they might have a mutiny on their hands. The crisis reached a critical point back at the army camp in Newburgh, New York, when on March 10, 1783, two anonymous addresses were circulated among the officers. One called for a meeting of officers to seek a "redress of grievances," while the other told officers that they had to stand up to a country that "tramples upon your rights, disdains your cries and insults your distresses." If officers threatened to refuse to disband following a formal declaration of peace, they could put pressure on Congress to have their demands met. By all accounts, George Washington was instrumental in quieting the crisis when he called a meeting of officers and warned them not to "lessen the dignity, and sully the glory you have hitherto maintained." He promised to support their complaints, and advocate on their behalf to Congress, and after the meeting the officers affirmed their loyalty to Congress. Following this episode, Congress agreed to the officer's principal demand of commutation by giving them five years' full pay in the form of government securities that promised 6 percent annual interest.[73]

Commutation was very unpopular in Massachusetts and throughout New England. Many people believed that much had already been sacrificed to provide for soldiers and officers in the Continental army, and some were upset that the amount of the bonus—equivalent to five years full pay—represented a greater amount of time than many officers had actually served. Others decried the fact that officers were promised this bonus, while enlisted men received nothing. Many others also resented the fact that this bonus seemed to have been the fruit of extortion and threats, because Congress felt pressured to give in to the officers' demands voiced and barely contained in Newburgh. Perhaps the biggest concern, however, was that Congress's promise of commutation had added again to the federal debt, and it created another pool of creditors who were promised regular interest payments and considerable principal.[74]

Concern over commutation was blunted by the emerging news of formal peace with Great Britain and the end of the war. People in Massachusetts looked forward to the official end of the war and hoped that the economy would stabilize and an economic recovery would follow. Before the war, New England had carried on a robust trade with Great Britain's colonies in the West Indies, providing fish, timber, and corn in exchange for sugar, molasses, rum, and bills of exchange from sugar planters that could be used to settle accounts with English merchants. Of course, such trade had been impossible during the war, but after the Treaty of Paris was signed, Britain refused to allow New England merchants to trade with its colonies in the West Indies. Merchants made efforts to expand into other markets, but the loss of an important trading partner combined with the renewed sale of English goods in Massachusetts following the war created a trade deficit, which meant that a great deal of gold and silver coin left the state to pay for foreign goods. In the first years of the war, the problem had been inflation caused by the high demand for food and supplies for armies and a flood of paper currency. As early as 1781, however, a growing problem was deflation, which had begun when the state legislature reduced the supply of paper money but dramatically increased because of the trade deficit. The deflationary economy meant that prices for farm products, as well as real and personal property, fell. Deflation was especially damaging for those in debt, whether they owed money to a merchant or to the government in taxes. In the early 1780s, the number of legal suits against debtors increased dramatically, especially in central and western Massachusetts.[75]

Individual debtors still did what they could to hold on to their property in such difficult times. If they had a close relationship with the creditor, or if the creditor was not facing pressure to pay his own debts, the debtor might be able to convince his creditor to give him more time to pay. Desperate debtors resorted not only to individual appeals but occasionally to collective efforts to prevent enforcement. In Hampshire County in 1783, a group of sixty men tried to prevent the court at Springfield from holding its session in May of 1783. Described in one newspaper account as "a banditti, collected from the obscure corners of the county," the men assembled at a tavern where they drew up a list of grievances, which they planned to present to the court. They assembled under an elm tree next to the courthouse, where they armed themselves "with white bludgeons, cut for the purpose." They marched to the door of the courthouse, where they told the sheriff that they wanted the court to adjourn. When the sheriff refused, a fight broke out between the insurgents and other bystanders who supported the court. After "the mob was repulsed with broken heads," some were arrested.[76] The arrested men later petitioned for clemency by stating that they had been unable to pay taxes because of "the great Scarcity of current Money and other Embarrassments arising from their Exertions in the late War."[77] Another incident took place in the Worcester County town of Sutton, when a group of men joined others from the nearby town of Douglass to form a "Mob to Resist authority and the Dew oppration of the Law."[78]

Of course, it was not just individual debtors who faced their creditors. Both the state of Massachusetts and the Confederation Congress had debts to pay, and in order to make good on these debts, the state government continued to press for the enforcement of tax collection, while also authorizing new direct taxes in 1783 and 1784. The tax of 1783 levied a total of £200,000, nearly 40 percent of which was earmarked to pay interest on government securities.[79] The tax of 1784 levied £140,000 more payable in outstanding army notes.[80] While the legislature worked to ensure that all taxes were collected as quickly as possible, some cautioned the state to not press its authority too far. In Springfield's *Hampshire Herald* in September 1784, an editorial noted that the real estate of seven tax collectors was being advertised for sale in Springfield. The county sheriff had seized their property because of taxes that had gone uncollected. According to this writer, the inability to collect the taxes was not based on laziness or negligence, for the collectors had "taken and exposed to sale cattle, and other property, belonging not merely to the poorer people, but to substantial farmers." This had happened because "money had flown away" and "the farmer and mechanic find no means to procure it." This distress had not yet caused a major uprising, "but you may hear the deep sigh of perplexity; you may see the sad face of desperation." State authorities had to be careful not to push the people too hard, or they could see the "powers of Government . . . burst asunder."[81]

## 2  Governor Bowdoin Faces
the Regulators

FROM THE RATIFICATION of the state constitution until the spring of 1785, each annual election for governor of Massachusetts was won handily by Boston merchant John Hancock. However, by the beginning of 1785, Hancock was tiring of the position. In addition to suffering from gout, he faced ongoing criticism from political rivals in Boston who sought to end his control of the governorship. In February, Hancock abruptly resigned, setting the stage for a competitive election for governor. A three-way race developed between former lieutenant governor Thomas Cushing (a political ally of Hancock who had replaced him after his resignation), former secretary of war Benjamin Lincoln, and merchant James Bowdoin. None of the three candidates received a majority of the popular vote, and so the election moved to the legislature. While a majority of the lower house favored Cushing, a majority of the state senate voted for Bowdoin, making him governor on May 26, 1785.[1]

James Bowdoin and John Hancock had much in common. Both were part of wealthy merchant families; Hancock's father died when Hancock was a young boy, but he was raised by his uncle, who was perhaps mid-eighteenth-century Boston's most prominent merchant. Both Bowdoin and Hancock attended Harvard before entering the family business, and both became involved in politics in the years leading up to the revolution. As a member of the Governor's Council in the 1760s and early 1770s, Bowdoin became increasingly critical of British economic policy, while Hancock became a hero to colonial protestors and later a leading patriot in Boston after he was charged by the British with smuggling in 1768. When war threatened, Bowdoin was chosen as one of the representatives to the Continental Congress, but poor health influenced his decision to stay home, and Hancock was chosen in his place. Bowdoin later served as the president of the 1780 state Constitutional Convention and worked closely with John and Samuel Adams to shape and champion the document. But despite their similarities, the two became political rivals. Both men actively pursued the governorship in 1780, but Hancock prevailed, and then Bowdoin refused to accept the position of lieutenant governor. Now, after nearly five years, James Bowdoin would have a chance to lead the state of Massachusetts.[2]

## Bowdoin's Vision

Upon taking office on June 2, 1785, Bowdoin attempted to lay out his vision of a peaceful and prosperous state in an address to both houses of the legislature in Boston. He began by reminding his audience that winning independence and creating a legitimate and viable framework of government had required a great deal of struggle and sacrifice, and those gains had to be protected at all costs. Bowdoin called upon citizens to remain vigilant and be willing to defend the state's constitution against any threat.[3] He then identified the imbalance of foreign trade as a major problem that had to be addressed. Manufactured goods from Great Britain and other European countries were pouring into Massachusetts, but it had been difficult for the state's goods to find a market overseas. Bowdoin supported changes to the Articles of Confederation that would give the central government more authority to regulate trade, and his hope was that in the long term a coherent and unified national trade policy could be an effective response to the current trade deficit. Until that happened, Bowdoin told his listeners that it was up to them "to remedy the evils, of which the merchant, the tradesman and manufacturer, and indeed every other description of persons among us, so justly complain." For Bowdoin, the short-term solution was for all Americans to "adopt a plan of frugality and economy." If the people of Massachusetts bought fewer manufactured goods, it would limit their own personal debt while helping to reduce the overall trade deficit. The effort to cut expenses would produce the "happy effect" of making Americans less interested in goods that Bowdoin believed were "superfluous and unnecessary." For Bowdoin, it was a desire for unneeded goods—and not the trade policy of the British or anyone else— that was "the principal source of our difficulties."[4]

After arguing that undisciplined habits of consumption were behind the Bay State's economic downturn, Bowdoin linked the economic behavior of individuals to the financial situation of the state as a whole. Just like individual debtors, the state had to get its house in order by reducing expenses, and by ensuring that it scrupulously paid its creditors on time and in full. Only by following such "principles of honour and strict honesty" would the state restore its public credit and be able to borrow money in the future. To achieve this goal, Bowdoin recommended creating a fund "for the regular payment of a considerable part of the interest of the public debt," which would allow "within a reasonable time" to lessen and finally eliminate the state debt.[5] Of course, under such a plan, those (like Governor Bowdoin himself) who owned state government securities could count on prompt and regular interest payments, and the market value of their securities would also increase. However, creating such a fund would require new revenue. Massachusetts had levied direct taxes in 1783 and 1784, and in the spring before Bowdoin's election in 1785 the legislature had authorized a Stamp Act that taxed newspapers, almanacs, and business and legal papers. But Bowdoin was suggesting that those measures would not be enough.[6]

As the new governor of Massachusetts, Bowdoin was in a good position to share his vision in an effort to shape the economic policy of the commonwealth in the mid-1780s. And while his views might not have been shared by a majority of people in the state, they were supported by a significant number of prominent men (and women) both within the state and in the rest of the United States. While it is true that at least some of this support came from people who owned state securities and therefore stood to profit personally from Bowdoin's policies, it is also true that others supported Bowdoin because they believed that tackling the state debt as soon as possible was the best way to ensure future economic prosperity and political stability. This perspective was partially shaped by a revolutionary tradition that emphasized self-sacrifice for a common good, but it was also informed by newer ideas that championed the role that commerce could play in the growth of the new nation. Prominent merchants and lawyers like Pennsylvania's Robert Morris and New York's Alexander Hamilton believed that higher taxes would stimulate economic activity because in order to pay their taxes more isolated farmers would need to produce more items that could be made available for sale to more distant markets. And if agricultural production increased and those additional products found buyers overseas, then America's trade deficit would be reduced and more money would flow into the states from abroad. While such views were common among elites, they also were persuasive to commercially oriented farmers, artisans, and others who lived in areas like the Atlantic coast or the Connecticut River valley where long-distance trade was a central part of economic life.[7]

While the Massachusetts legislature discussed the issues raised by Bowdoin, the Confederation Congress spent the summer of 1785 at its then current home in New York City working on a new requisition request for the states. Since 1781, Congress had tried unsuccessfully to amend the Articles of Confederation to give the central government the direct authority to raise revenue by taxing foreign imports. However, because such a change required unanimous consent of all thirteen states, the opposition of Rhode Island in 1781 and New York in 1783 were enough to prevent the changes from taking effect. Therefore, the federal government was forced to continue to rely on requisitions of funds from the states. Periodic requisitions had been made in the 1780s, but the problem from the perspective of many in Congress was that states were not compelled to meet these requisitions. As a result, the federal Congress was chronically short of revenue and had increasing difficulty simply meeting its interest payments, both to domestic creditors and to Dutch bankers and the French government.[8] For much of 1785, Congress labored to produce and craft a new requisition request of $3 million, which it presented to the states in late September.[9] While some of this money was to go to foreign creditors, a significant portion was intended for domestic creditors, including those who held "Commutation certificates," the government paper that was issued to Continental army officers in the wake of the Newburgh Conspiracy.[10]

After Governor Bowdoin received the news of this requisition, he informed the Massachusetts legislature that the state was expected to submit slightly more than $488,000 by May 1786 in order to meet its share of the $3 million total. Over and above the obligations posed by the requisition, Bowdoin reminded the legislature that the total state debt was more than £1.4 million (or roughly $4.6 million), which required annual interest payments of more than £88,000 (or more than $293,000).[11] Back in 1781, the legislature had directed that the proceeds of the state's impost and excise taxes go directly to pay this interest, but according to Bowdoin such taxes in the past year had brought less than £60,000. As a result, it was unlikely that taxes on imports alone would cover the interest payments, and in addition to levying a direct tax to pay for the federal requisition, the state would also need direct tax income to support interest payments to the state's creditors.[12]

Bowdoin's call for a new round of direct taxes was combined with an emphasis on prompt tax collection. While state officials had made considerable efforts to hold tax collectors accountable, it was still the case that none of the state taxes levied since 1780 had been paid in full. As Governor Bowdoin reported, "There is a large sum now due for past taxes." Bowdoin signaled that enforcement of tax levies was very important, and that more efficient tax collection was a necessity. According to Bowdoin, "Punctuality in the payment of taxes is so essential to public credit, that the existence of the latter depends upon it." In his address to the legislature, Bowdoin recommended that it pass a law authorizing interest penalties on taxes that were not paid on time and in full, while those who paid on time would get a 5 percent reduction in their tax. For Bowdoin, such a rule would be a "stimulus to punctuality," and it would provide for a more just and efficient tax system.[13]

Four days after this address, Bowdoin made the legislature aware of more bad news from the Confederation Congress. Not only had it issued a new requisition, but it still sought the full returns from previous requisitions in 1781 and 1782. The state of Massachusetts had already paid considerable sums, but it had not completely met those earlier requisitions. As a result, Bowdoin said, the actual amount that the state should submit to the Confederation Congress was not $488,000 but rather $931,615.66.[14] Massachusetts was not alone; while every state had responded to previous requisitions by levying different taxes, no state had come close to meeting all of its federal requisition demands.[15] For a while, Congress had been able to make interest payments on its debts thanks to continued foreign loans, "but those funds being now wholly exhausted, the sole reliance of Congress is on the prompt and vigorous exertions of the several States, to answer the requisition." For Bowdoin, this was a serious situation that threatened the very survival of the fledgling union: without prompt and significant payments by the states, the very "dignity, operations and existence" of the federal government were at stake. Given how desperate the situation was, Bowdoin urged the legislature "to take the most speedy and the most vigorous measures to comply with those several requisitions."[16] In December 1785, Bowdoin passed along one additional warning from the Confederation Congress. The governor had received word "that the funds in the treasury are scarcely sufficient to defray the daily incidental charges." Even more upsetting, interest payments were due to Dutch bankers in February, June, and November, and there were no funds to meet those interest payments. If the Confederation Congress failed to make those payments, "our credit with Holland in particular . . . will be inevitably destroyed."[17]

## Calls for Relief

From Bowdoin, the message was clear and consistent: the only way to respond to the currency shortage was to buy fewer imports and work harder to produce exports, and the only way to respond to sizable wartime debts was to require substantial taxes rigorously collected and prompt payment of interest to creditors, both foreign and domestic. Bowdoin's prescription would receive a warm reception among many in the state legislature, who considered it the only way to maintain the "dignity and honour" of government. Some, like Bowdoin, were merchants and creditors themselves, or like Samuel Adams they shared a belief that self-sacrifice was the only legitimate way to preserve the republic. Others in the state, however, held a different view. In order to solve the problem of limited currency, many started to argue that, rather than taking the slow, indirect, and uncertain route of stopping imports and expanding exports, the government should directly increase the money supply by printing paper currency. At the same time that Bowdoin was trying to convince the state legislature to support higher taxes, petitions calling for paper money began to arrive from farming communities from across the interior of the state, and a steady stream of such petitions continued through the winter and spring of 1786. Nearly all of these petitions came from the three western counties of Berkshire, Hampshire, and Worcester, or from Plymouth County, located between Boston and Rhode Island.[18]

In addition to mounting interest in paper money, there was also a growing concern that while high taxes helped maintain the creditworthiness of the state, the real beneficiaries of such taxes were public creditors. For men like Bowdoin, self-sacrifice for the common good meant a reduced consumption of luxury goods and the prompt payment of taxes. Others believed in self-sacrifice for the greater good, but they questioned whether the calls for sacrifice had been fairly distributed. Throughout the decade, high taxes had led to numerous sheriff's sales, as delinquent taxpayers were forced to hand over livestock and other property. Some began to wonder if the cost was too high and if perhaps creditors should share in the sacrifice by having their interest payments delayed or reduced. As one writer argued in the Boston newspaper the *Massachusetts Centinel*, the holders of public debt had often bought such securities for pennies on the dollar. It would not punish that creditor, therefore, if interest on the securities was not determined by the *face* value but rather by the *market* value of such paper: "A redemption at the current depreciated value is neither injustice, nor breach of faith."[19]

As it stood, creditors who had purchased securities at a fraction of their face value but who were receiving 6 percent interest on the *face value* were making very large returns on their investment. As the *Massachusetts Centinel* writer put it, "There are many things in government, which people in general have neither leisure to examine, nor capacity to comprehend," and therefore they have to leave it up to the legislature's "wisdom and integrity." However, other matters could be understood by everyone, and in those cases the people should express their opinion. Interest payments on the state debt, this writer believed, was one of those issues. Because of speculation in government securities, most of the holders were effectively making 20 or 30 percent interest, rather than 5 or 6: "The simple peasant sees, as plainly as the profoundest politician, that FIVE is less than TWENTY." For this writer, it made no sense for the government to pay such high rates of interest.[20]

The argument against paying interest at face value was perhaps most forcefully articulated by a writer calling himself "Old Soldier," who penned a short personal history of the American Revolution that was printed in several Massachusetts newspapers. When the American Revolution began, "Old Solider" joined many of his fellow countrymen who dropped what they were doing, left their families, and went to fight for independence. "Old Soldier" was a farmer, and he "left with regret my little farm." It had not made him wealthy, but it had provided him and his family "a competency," that is, enough to meet their basic needs. As the war continued, he was anxious to return home to be with his family and run his farm, which he had left under the supervision "of a young man, whom I promised to reward with the wages that were to be allowed me from government." However, he remained in the army until America was "seated on the throne of Independence." In exchange for his service, he received "my country's solemn promises of a satisfactory reward." When the war finally ended, the government was forced to pay the soldiers in notes because of the "exhausted state of our finances," which they accepted "without a murmur." However, once he returned home, he found that both the man he hired to work the farm and the local merchant "refused payment in these securities at the rate at which I took them of government." He felt that this was unfair, but the needs of his family compelled him to sell his government notes for one-quarter their value. Now, the "Old Soldier" was appalled that those who currently held the notes were benefiting from the difficult sacrifices people made to pay their taxes. Rather than serving in the army, the "Old Soldier" charged that these creditors had "sauntered at home during the war, enjoying the smiles of fortune, wallowing in affluence, and fattening in the ease of sunshine and prosperity." The thought that he and his "little farm" would be taxed to benefit these creditors made him angry: *"Forbid it, humanity! forbid it, gratitude and justice!"*[21]

While some critics of the full funding of state debt emphasized the plight of the original holders of government notes, others focused on the perceived illegitimacy of the profits made by those who had purchased the notes from the original holders at a deep discount. One critic estimated that "perhaps nineteen parts in twenty of the publick securities are possessed by merchants and opulent gentlemen in the capital and other maritime towns." Under the current state law "every tax laid on the community is virtually a tax to them; the greater the debt, the greater is their gain; they are accumulating fortunes by the general distress." Perhaps as an allusion to Governor Bowdoin and other members of government who owned government securities, this writer noted that many public creditors could influence the decisions of the legislature and wondered if they would do the right thing and advocate for reducing the value of these securities for the good of the whole. The anonymous writer believed that they would, because "Gentlemen of their education and profession have generally the most enlarged and liberal views." Looking back on the struggle with Britain, this writer maintained that merchants and other prominent people were among those willing to "sacrifice the profits of their trade on the altar of liberty." Given that history, how could creditors "tarnish the glory of former patriotism by oppressing their fellow-citizens, or by opposing a measure necessary to general relief"?[22]

Besides calls to print paper money and possibly to reduce the value of the state debt, relief was sought in one other direct way. Back in 1782, in the wake of the Samuel Ely uprising, the legislature passed a law that allowed debtors to have the value of their property assessed by three people in the community rather than sold at auction, and therefore the value of the property seized would be greater than if it were offered at auction. Calls were again made to craft such legislation to provide some measure of relief to debtors. The calls for paper money and other relief measures upset many, especially those in more commercially oriented towns. Critics of paper money were quick to remind people of the runaway inflation of the 1770s, and they argued that any new emissions of paper would create a similar situation. In addition, most critics of paper money shrugged off the distress in the countryside and repeated that it was a ploy on the part of debtors to avoid making good on their obligations to creditors and tax collectors. As one writer noted, "Nothing is more easy than to procure petitions for any measure in which the petitioners themselves are self-interested, be the operation of that measure ever so injurious to the general weal of their country." He then lampooned the supporters of paper money by penning his own satirical petition stating that paper money advocates "preferred the borrowing of money . . . to the ignominious humiliation of working with their own hands." To drive home the point, the fake petition was signed by men with names like "Amos Spendthrift . . . Tom Seldomsober . . . & Simon Dreadwork."[23]

## The Legislature Chooses Sides

Between the fall of 1785 and the spring of 1786, the Massachusetts legislature had to chart a course between Governor Bowdoin's call for high taxes and protection of public creditors and petitions from the towns calling for paper money and other forms of tax and debt relief. In practically every way, the legislature sided with Governor Bowdoin. In the fall of 1785, legislators from farming communities in parts of central and western Massachusetts advocated a personal property tender law and an emission of paper currency. However, both measures were voted down by large margins. In early November, the state legislature voted 93-23 against a paper money proposal, and a personal property tender measure was also soundly defeated by a vote of 89-35.[24]

While that defeat spawned more town petitions for paper currency, which did lead to the formation of a legislative committee to reexamine the paper money issue, it and a personal property tender bill were again defeated in a vote on March 14, 1786.[25] Instead of passing any relief measures, the Massachusetts legislature pressed ahead with a significant new direct tax. On March 23, 1786, the legislature approved the largest direct tax of the decade, when it levied £300,439 to be paid in the next year. Half of the money was to pay for the federal requisition, and most of the rest was to pay interest on state debt. One-third of the tax would have to be paid in gold or silver coin, which is the first time since October 1781 that taxpayers in Massachusetts were required to pay any part of the direct tax in hard currency.[26]

In addition to levying new taxes, the legislature took steps to improve the efficiency of tax collection. In February 1786, it passed a law partially entitled "An act for enforcing the speedy payment of rates and taxes."[27] This legislation reorganized and clarified all existing laws on tax collection, authorized assessors to select new constables if the current ones were unable or unwilling to complete the collections, and also provided the state with recourse if the collector absconded without completing his collection. The legislature also streamlined collection accounting by requiring collectors to provide updates to the state treasurer every two months and by obliging the town selectmen to periodically check in with the constable to ensure that collection was progressing.[28]

Throughout the 1780s, enforcement of tax collection had been the responsibility of county sheriffs, who had the discretion to not follow through with actions against collectors. Some county sheriffs, like Loammi Baldwin in Middlesex County, vigorously enforced strict collection and arrested or seized property from lax town collectors. Others, like Sheriff Caleb Hyde from Berkshire County, were much less likely to take action against delinquent collectors. By the spring of 1786, Sheriff Hyde had not enforced treasurer's executions for more than £11,000 from taxes going back to 1781. In early summer, the legislature asked the governor to investigate Hyde's conduct, suggesting that he was not fulfilling his duty as sheriff. Then, in early July, the legislature took away the discretion of sheriffs like Hyde and made them personally responsible for any taxes that went uncollected in their county. The resolve noted that demands from the state treasurer to county sheriffs to force delinquent collectors to make good on their collections had been "repeatedly returned unsatisfied, or satisfied in part only." Because such inaction was no longer acceptable to the legislature, it authorized the county coroner to seize any sheriff who failed to collect all of the taxes on treasury executions. So that people throughout the commonwealth were aware of this change, the legislature directed that it be published in two newspapers in Boston, along with the papers in Plymouth, Newburyport, Worcester, Springfield, and Cumberland.[29]

In following the course of action recommended by Bowdoin, the Massachusetts legislature sought to raise enough tax revenue to simultaneously pay the interest of both state and federal creditors. Other New England states did not choose this ambitious path. In New Hampshire, the state legislature decided to delay interest payments on state loan certificates in order to attempt to pay its share of the federal requisition. Connecticut also made a choice, ultimately refusing to pay its share of the federal requisition, in an effort to meet its own debts.[30] In Rhode Island, the legislature had authorized a direct tax of £20,000 in the summer of 1785 in anticipation of the federal requisition. This tax proved wildly unpopular in rural communities outside of Rhode Island port towns, and these communities organized in the spring of 1786 to elect representatives that radically changed the composition of state government. Incumbents, including the governor and half of the senate, were voted out of office. The new legislature authorized an emission of paper money that citizens could use to pay their Continental taxes.[31]

Massachusetts also had annual elections in the spring of 1786, but those in the countryside who advocated relief measures were unable to mobilize as effectively as their Rhode Island neighbors had. In fact, some interior towns that had been represented in 1785 failed to elect or send a representative for the new legislative session that began in late May 1786. It appears that some towns refused to send representatives as an act of protest, while others may have figured that it was not worth the expense to send a representative to a legislature that had signaled strong and sustained opposition to relief measures.[32] When a paper money bill was presented in June, it was defeated by an even more lopsided majority than had been the case the previous November. The summer session ended with no substantive legislation aimed to provide relief to debtors or taxpayers, and the legislature decided that it would not hold a fall session but rather wait until January of 1787 before reconvening.[33]

## Return of the County Conventions

Even before the legislative session ended on July 8, representatives from many of the towns in Bristol County (located near Rhode Island) had decided to meet in a county convention at the Taunton courthouse, and on June 27 the convention sent a petition to the state legislature. This petition identified some of the crucial issues plaguing the people of the county, and it asked for significant relief efforts. Despite the fact that recent legislative votes concerning paper currency bills had showed that the majority of the legislature was opposed to such a measure, the Bristol County convention called for an emission of paper money. It argued that in most places in the state, "except Boston and a few towns adjacent," the lack of currency was causing a great deal of distress. It had made the tax obligations of most people difficult if not impossible to meet, and it was such a burden that it threatened "to make us a miserable, cruel-hearted, and wicked people." The representatives in the Bristol convention recognized the criticisms of paper money; namely, that debtors could engage in a kind of fraud by paying off their debts in paper money that was worth less than the actual value of their debts. But those who met in Taunton had the following response: "As to the fraud of depreciation, we are in no wise afraid that the fraud or cheat will be equal to that fraud or cheat now made upon the people by means of the scarcity of hard money, by which property is taken by distress from the people for a trifle." They also responded to the critique that if only people worked more diligently, they would be able to pay their taxes and get out of debt. They believed that in general "people are very industrious in every part of the Commonwealth." They admitted that there were a few exceptions to this general rule; however, those could be found "mostly about sea-ports and market-places."[34] In addition to requesting paper money, the convention also asked the legislature for two more direct kinds of relief: first, until the amount of money in circulation increased, there should be "a suspension of law in all civil cases." In other words, the Court of Common Pleas, which was the civil court that handled debt cases, should not meet, which would allow distressed debtors to hold on to their property. Personal debts would not be forgiven, but debtors would be assured that their property would not be taken. Second, the convention requested that no direct taxes be collected at all for a period of nine months.[35]

The state legislature took no action on the Bristol County petition before adjourning for six months. Almost immediately, another Bristol County convention representing eight towns again met in Taunton, but instead of addressing the legislature, they reached out to "the INHABITANTS of the Commonwealth of MASSACHUSETTS." The address began by making a claim for the legitimacy of country conventions and other such meetings: "In a time of public distress it is the right as well as the duty of a people to enquire impartially into the measures leading to oppression." Therefore, they came together and "calmly and seriously enquired" into the cost of government, which they said was a fundamental reason why people were upset, because it was "far beyond the ability of the people" to pay for. The Bristol conventioneers suggested only a couple of specific changes. First, they believed that the Constitution be revised to abolish the state senate, which they considered "a useless and unnecessary branch of government." They also wanted greater control over the salaries paid to government officials, and so they suggested that officials' salaries should be "annually dependent on the people." That would give the people "command of our property," and it might allow them to get a relatively quick response to their grievances, instead of "depending upon despised petitions." Rather than provide any other specific remedies, the Bristol convention spoke directly to the citizens and declared that the state's problems "must excite you" to organize other county conventions. It hoped there might be a call for "a COMMONWEALTH CONVENTION, to collect the sentiments of the inhabitants" of the whole state and to work on revising the state's constitution.[36]

Just like previous county conventions, the convention movement of the summer of 1786 sparked considerable criticism of both the content of its proposals—especially the call for paper money—and the form of its protest. For example, writing in the *Worcester Magazine* at the end of August, "An American" called into question the right of the Bristol towns to call a convention, as well as the concerns that were at the center of the meeting. While the members of the convention were convinced that the short supply of paper money had led to significant distress in the countryside, "An American" dismissed such concerns. He doubted whether the conditions were as bad in the countryside as the convention members believed, and even if they were, it was due to the farmer's lack of effort: "Temperance, frugality and industry, will infallibly ensure a competence in this county—While indolence and dissipation must inevitably produce an opposite effect." This writer believed that critics of the government were causing disorder and commotion for no good reason, and as a result they were failing as fathers and as men: "The man who spends that time in unavailing complaints, which should be devoted to the support of his family, must be sure to suffer."[37]

These criticisms of county conventions would grow as the movement did. When the towns of Cambridge and Medford were invited to attend the Middlesex County convention, they refused and published the reasons why they did so. A circular letter sent from Boston argued not only that such meetings were unnecessary and unwise but that they smacked of sedition: "We are convinced that the present disturbances arise from British emissaries, residing among us, whose every wish is for our overthrow and ruin; or from the machinations of wicked and unprincipled men" who sought to use the disturbances for their own personal political or financial gain.[38]

Such criticisms of county conventions served to further alienate some champions of debt and tax relief. One such supporter of relief, a man named George Brock from the town of Attleboro, became furious at the opposition to the convention movement. He noted that rather than carefully considering the petitions for relief, the legislature had treated them "with supreme contempt." Instead of recognizing that the convention movement was a sign of genuine distress, the legislature and its allies believed that the people were "luxurious in their diet, idle and profligate in their manners, encouragers of foreign manufacturers." In the countryside, Brock argued, so many people were in such dire straits that talk about overspending on luxuries was ridiculous. Instead of buying unneeded items, many people in the countryside were having trouble just making enough for bare subsistence, and unless the legislature wanted the people to "follow the example of the oppressed Irish, and live wholly on skimed milk and potatoes," Brock was not certain how people could long continue given the current conditions. Rather than being seen as vigilant defenders of freedom, convention supporters were stigmatized as "traitors, incendiaries, vile creatures" who were "threatened . . . with prosecutions for daring to inquire into the present gross mismanagement of our rulers."[39]

Many in the countryside shared Brock's belief that conventions were legitimate, and the Bristol convention meetings were followed by separate conventions in Middlesex, Worcester, Hampshire, and Berkshire counties in late August. In Hampshire County, representatives from fifty of the county's fifty-eight towns met in town of Hatfield for four days starting on August 22. (By comparison, only twenty-seven Hampshire towns had sent representatives to Boston for the start of the May 1786, legislative session.) At the end of the meetings, the convention members agreed to a list of twenty-five articles. As the Bristol convention had done, they identified issues that needed to be addressed in order to provide relief to debtors and taxpayers, including the salaries of government officials, the cost of legal fees and taxes, and interest payments to government bond holders. They recommended that towns in the county instruct their representatives to support paper currency legislation. Rather than wait until January, they wanted the governor to call for the legislature to assemble immediately. In addition, like their fellow convention delegates in Bristol, those at the Hatfield convention also recommended revising the state constitution: "Whereas several of the above articles of grievances, arise from defects in the constitution; therefore a revision of the same ought to take place."[40]

While this convention suggested a significant departure from recent financial policy, it took pains to emphasize that it sought to operate within the bounds of the law, and it called for all people to "abstain from all mobs and unlawful assemblies, until a constitutional method of redress can be obtained."[41] The positions taken by the Hatfield convention were not universally supported in Hampshire County. The representatives who had come to Hatfield had been chosen through town meetings, and they brought these convention results back to their towns. Towns then discussed the convention's statement, and while many seemed to be in full support, others failed to agree with all of the recommendations. Both Hatfield and Springfield did not agree to instruct their representatives to work for a paper money law, and Springfield did not support a call to revise the Constitution. One of the few towns that did not send a representative to the convention, the market town of Northampton, was opposed to practically all of the recommendations made by the convention.[42]

## The Emergence of the Regulators

Four days after the end of the Hatfield convention, a Hampshire County court session was scheduled to take place in the town of Northampton, and on the eve of the session men began to gather in towns from across the county before converging on the courthouse. The next morning, the men—estimated at upward of fifteen hundred, with at least five hundred shouldering guns—marched to fife and drum and paraded in front of the courthouse.

Later that morning, the county sheriff Elisha Porter led the three court judges toward the courthouse, but when they encountered the throng of men they decided to retreat to a nearby tavern, where they were joined by a six-man delegation representing the crowd. The insurgents wanted no court business transacted until the people's grievances had been redressed: "If your Honours will be so kind as to compare the Grants of the Legislature to the officers of Government & Salaries that are established by Law with the principles of the Constitution & the present Circumstances of the good People of this Commonwealth & also consider the great Scarcity of Cash we have not the least Doubt but that your Honours upon a serious Consideration will join us in Sentiment."[43] No organized support for the judges appeared, and recognizing that they had no choice, the judges agreed to adjourn the court session. Once that decision was made, the armed crowd dispersed. One bystander who was opposed to the crowd's actions nevertheless recognized their order and organization: the men behaved "with less insolence and violence, and with more sobriety and good order, than is commonly to be expected in such a large and promiscuous assembly, collected in so illegal a manner, and for so unwarrantable a purpose."[44]

Immediately following the court closure, Sheriff Porter informed Governor Bowdoin of the news. Other court sessions were scheduled in the next couple of weeks in Worcester, Berkshire, Middlesex, and Bristol counties, and the governor was uncertain how to proceed. The legislature was not in session, and most of the members of his own council were not in Boston. For legal advice, the governor met on September 1 with two judges known as stalwart defenders of government authority and prerogative, Theophilus Parsons of Newburyport and David Sewall of York. Bowdoin sought their legal advice regarding how law enforcement officials might respond to the threat of a court closure. Parsons told Bowdoin that it was his legal opinion that any crowd that tried to intimidate judges into not holding a court session were guilty of an unlawful assembly and could therefore be arrested by the sheriff or his deputies. Parsons believed that intimidation took place if the crowd came armed "with muskets, swords, clubs, or weapons of offence," or if they blocked the path to the courthouse and prevented the judges from entering. The sheriff should attempt to use "peaceable methods" to command the crowd to disperse, but if the crowd refused, Parsons believed that it was the sheriff's duty "to use the necessary force," and it was the right of the sheriff to fire upon the crowd in order to support the sitting of the court. Parsons went

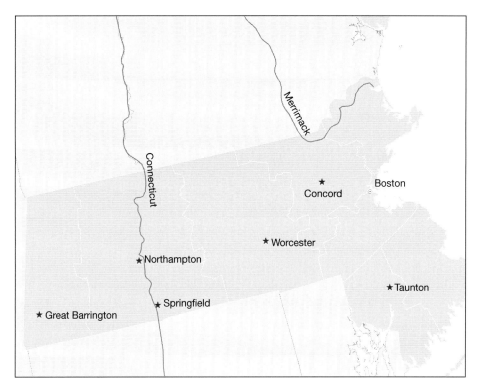

Towns in Massachusetts experiencing court closures in the fall of 1786.

on to say that if the state militia had been called out to support the sheriff, it was "bound to obey him," and it would also be justified in firing upon any crowd that attempted to prevent a court session from taking place.[45]

The next day, the governor issued a proclamation strongly condemning the closure of the Hampshire County court, and warned the people of Massachusetts that additional court closures would be dealt with harshly. He noted that many in the crowd had been "armed with guns, swords, and other deadly weapons" and that they marched "in contempt and open defiance of the authority of this Government." For Bowdoin, such action was never acceptable, because it threatened to "subvert all law and government . . . dissolve our excellent Constitution, and introduce universal riot, anarchy and confusion." The likely result, according to the governor, would be the end of the republic and the formation of an "absolute despotism." In order to avoid such a result, Bowdoin called upon all government officials, from judges to constables, to do everything in their power "to prevent and suppress all such violent and riotous proceedings."[46]

In addition to calling for the support of government officials, Bowdoin also spoke directly to the citizens of the state, urging them to remember that Massachusetts had purchased its liberty and independence at great cost, and that they would need to act in order to ensure that they would pass on to their children a state of "peace, freedom, and safety" rather than "anarchy, confusion, and slavery." He hoped that all citizens would actively support government officials "in preventing and suppressing all . . . treasonable proceedings, and every measure that has a tendency to encourage them." Finally, Bowdoin authorized the state's attorney general, Robert Treat Paine, to "prosecute and bring to condign punishment the Ringleaders and Abettors of the aforesaid atrocious violation of Law and government" and to approach future violations in the same way. "Condign punishment" meant that Paine should seek to impose the appropriate sentence for the crime, which Bowdoin had defined as a "treasonable" proceeding. For Bowdoin, therefore, those men who forcibly closed the court should be arrested, charged, and, if found guilty of treason, executed. Following the Ely uprising in 1782, the state government responded with clemency toward those who had acted with Ely to close the court, free him from jail, and face off against those government forces mobilized to recapture him. With this stern address, Bowdoin attempted to signal that the government response to similar uprisings would be much less forgiving.[47]

After issuing a public proclamation, the governor also communicated with sheriff and militia commanders to warn them of possible crowd action and to encourage them to organize support for the officers of the court. In Worcester County, the next court session was scheduled to open on September 5, so Bowdoin communicated with the local militia commander, General Jonathan Warner. Bowdoin told Warner that if the county sheriff should request support, he should provide as many troops as the sheriff thought necessary "to suppress any such attempt" to close the court.[48] Warner replied to the governor the next day and assured him that he had ordered several colonels in the militia to prepare themselves in case they were needed. Warner agreed that such troops would likely be needed "as the people in general are grown very clamorous & have not patience to wait for a regular redress of their real or supposed grievances."[49]

As it turned out, several hundred protesters were able to close the court in

Worcester, and none of the men called out to defend the court were willing to do so. In the aftermath of this crowd action, Shrewsbury resident Joseph Henshaw wrote to the governor to explain why he thought the militia had failed to materialize. Henshaw believed that once the crowd opposed to the court had formed and taken a defensive position, any militia force would be loath to take action against such a crowd. According to Henshaw, "it was exceedingly irksome to march in hostile array & shed the blood of their townsmen." For this reason he encouraged the governor to have a militia force organized and in place before any crowd had a chance to form: "Had three or four hundred of the militia been previously placed to guard the Court House & support the Court previous to the collection of the Mob, it is humbly presumed the case would have been otherwise as the militia would have been the defendants, and the mob the opponents."[50]

Upon hearing the upsetting news from Worcester, Bowdoin quickly called an informal meeting of some members of his council as well as other prominent political leaders, and this group met for four days beginning on September 7. This impromptu council included the prominent state senators Samuel Adams, and Samuel and William Phillips, along with several state Supreme Court justices, including Chief Justice William Cushing and Attorney General Robert Treat Paine. Also present was one member of the Governor's Council, Benjamin Austin, along with several state representatives from Boston (but none from areas where crowd actions had taken place).[51] This group did not form to consider any measures that might respond to the distress in the countryside; instead, they met to determine how to ensure that upcoming court sessions were defended. On September 12, county court sessions were scheduled for Taunton in Bristol County, Concord in Middlesex County, and Great Barrington in Berkshire County. The men counseled Bowdoin to call the legislature back into session earlier than planned, and then they debated sending a militia force to Concord. Bowdoin communicated with Middlesex County militia commander General Brooks, who warned Bowdoin that he was not sure how many Middlesex militia might turn out to support the court session. On September 9, Bowdoin and his informal advisers decided that they would call out militia from Boston and the surrounding communities of Roxbury and Dorchester—where support of the government was most clear—and send those forces to Concord. The next day, however, Bowdoin and his advisers were joined by two of the judges of Middlesex County, who asked that, rather than sending troops, the governor offer some kind of lenient measures to appease the disaffected. This plea led to debate and disagreement among Bowdoin's advisers; meanwhile, a messenger from Middlesex County arrived with word that a county convention was planning to negotiate with the men opposed to the opening of the court. On hearing this news, Bowdoin decided to countermand his order to nearby militia and hoped that the citizens of Middlesex could reach a peaceful solution on their own.[52]

As Bowdoin met in Boston, town leaders in Concord worried that the presence of insurgents and militia troops could lead to violence when the court opened there on September 12. On September 9 they held a special town meeting to call for a county convention for the day of the court session and sent word to other towns and to the governor. Before the planned court session, a circular letter was sent to encourage towns to send a representative to that convention. The letter declared the town's disapproval of the behavior of the protestors in Hampshire and Worcester, and even though it recognized the need to address real grievances, it maintained that protests had to be within the bounds of the law. They considered any intimidation or threat of violence on the part of the protestors to be unacceptable.[53] On the morning of September 12, the convention started meeting, and it formed one committee to meet with the court and another to meet with the insurgents.

While the county convention members gathered, a crowd of protestors also formed. When the county sheriff Loammi Baldwin arrived about ten o'clock in the morning, he found the members of the convention in Brown's tavern, while about seventy armed insurgents on Concord green tried to shelter themselves from a heavy rain. Baldwin said that he heard Captain Nathan Smith of the town of Shirley attempt to rally support with a passionate address. According to Baldwin, Smith "declare[d] aloud that every person who did not follow his drum and join the Regulators in two hours should be drove out of town at the point of the Bayonet."[54] Another account added that Smith told the men assembled, "As Christ laid down his life to save the world, so will I lay down my life to supress the government from all tirranical oppression, and you who are willing to join us in this hear affair may fall into our ranks. Those who do not after two hours, shall stand the monuments of God's sparing mercy."[55]

In addition to Smith, the other figure who seemed to command some authority among the insurgents was Job Shattuck, a fifty-year-old revolutionary war captain from the town of Groton who had held a number of town offices including selectman and constable. In 1781 Shattuck had been arrested after trying to prevent a neighbor's property from been seized as part of a debt suit, and he had played a role in the Middlesex convention movement to protest government policies. On this day in Concord, Shattuck arrived with eighty to one hundred men from Groton and surrounding towns. He brought a petition to the court officials in the early afternoon, asking them to adjourn without hearing any cases. In the petition, which was from "The voice of the people of this County," the court was asked to not meet until the people get a redress of grievances, "which will be set forth in a petition or remonstrance to the next General Court."[56] That afternoon, the "regulators" were joined by a group of men from Worcester County to the west, led by Captain Adam Wheeler of Hubbardstown.[57]

Many of the men from Worcester had likely taken part in the court closing there the previous week. After they arrived, and the two groups of insurgents discussed their plans, they all marched from the green over to the tavern, and then back to the green. Taking note of the size of the crowd, totaling between 250 and 300 insurgents now, the representatives from the county convention also came to the judges and urged them to capitulate in an effort to prevent violence. At first, the judges refused, telling the county convention representative Dr. Bartlett that because they were "held in Duress by a body of men in Arms, they neither would nor could act." Upon receiving that response, Dr. Bartlett refused to be the messenger to the crowd, telling the judges "that such was the temper of these people, that unless something was soon done they feared the House in which we were would be pulled down." According to one of the judges present, Samuel Phillips Savage, they then reluctantly agreed to give in to the demands of the regulators and adjourn the session of the court. Savage thought the whole affair was "humiliating" and called Shattuck's petition an insolent one, "which wounded the feelings of every Gentlemen present."[58]

Following the events in Concord, representatives of the Middlesex County convention agreed and, wanting to distance themselves from the actions of the crowd, told the governor that they "cannot forbear to express their disagreeable and painfull sensations that their endeavors to disuade from rash and unlawful measures have proved so ineffectual—They declare their utter abhorrence of the measures adopted by the body in arms & are fully sensible of the high criminality of which if not speedily prevented must unavoidably involve the Commonwealth in calamities innumerable & inexpressible."[59]

In Middlesex, the county convention was unable to prevent the "men at arms" from blocking the court session. Meanwhile, in Bristol County the militia commander Major General David Cobb told the governor that he was planning to gather a force to protect the courthouse before the session began. Bowdoin replied to Cobb with words of caution. He told him that he should not use violence, for fear of the consequences: "It is considered of the Utmost importance that no blood be shed on this Occasion." Bowdoin then went even further, noting that for some people "the very appearance of supporting the sitting of the Court by force of Arms will exasperate the Minds of many and give uneasiness to all the People."[60]

Despite the governor's words of cautious warning, Cobb did decide to call out the militia forces of Bristol and Plymouth counties to take possession of the courthouse before the insurgents had a chance to gather. According to Cobb, the militia was "happily in numbers sufficient to support the Civil Authority in the execution of Duty." In addition to loyal militia members, Cobb also secured the use of a cannon, which he placed right outside the courthouse door.[61] After the militia had clear control of the Taunton courthouse, "large numbers of People . . . many of whom were armed," also arrived. Despite the support and protection of the militia, the judges decided to adjourn the court until early December. They did this, Cobb believed, because "they conceived it to be their Duty to have some regard to the alarming disturbances of the present day."[62]

While opposition to court sessions in Concord and Taunton was unfolding, the county court in Berkshire County was also scheduled to meet. Back on September 2, Governor Bowdoin had written to militia commander Major General John Patterson to prepare the county militia to support the upcoming court session. After receiving the instructions from the governor, Patterson ordered his militia colonels to require all their men "to appear with their arms compleat at Great Barrington on Tuesday next at 9 oc[lock] in the morning."[63] On the morning of the court session, Patterson was able to lead an impressive militia force of about one thousand men into Great Barrington in support of the justices. However, when the men got near the courthouse, they realized that a crowd had already seized the courthouse, with the apparent intent of preventing the justices from entering.[64]

When the justices became aware of the situation, someone suggested that the militia forces be allowed to decide whom they wanted to support: they could stand on one side of the road to support the opening of the court or the other side of the road to support the regulators. According to eyewitnesses, between seven or eight hundred of the nearly one thousand militiamen sided with the regulators. The judges recognized that they could not hold a session under those circumstances, and so they adjourned to the home of Judge William Whiting. The insurgents followed them and demanded that they sign an agreement not to hold court "until the Constitution of the Government shall be revised or a new one made."[65] Three of the judges, including Whiting, signed the pledge. Only Judge Jaleel Woodbridge refused, saying that he would resign his commission before signing the pledge. After this, some of the insurgents marched to the jailhouse, where they freed the debtors housed there. According to one eyewitness, the regulators had traveled from nearly two dozen different towns from across Berkshire County, and although they armed themselves and forcibly prevented the court from opening, which "in the eye of law . . . amounts to Treason," they did not steal anything or destroy any property. In the town of Pittsfield, two of the insurgents got drunk but "were confined by their officers lest they should commit irregularities."[66]

In the space of a few weeks, crowds of men had converged on the civil court sessions in four counties from Bristol in the southeast to Berkshire in the far west. While many of these men came to the courthouse armed, they did not use violence to achieve their goal of closing the courts, but they did seek to intimidate public officials with the threat of force. They called themselves regulators, or a "body of the people," and they hoped their pressure would compel the government to reconsider relief for debtors and taxpayers. The term *regulator* or *the regulation* had been used by farmers in both North Carolina and South Carolina in the years before the American Revolution. Building on a tradition of rural protest that had its origins across the Atlantic in the seventeenth century, the regulators of North Carolina organized as crowds to intimidate and put pressure on courts and government officials when they believed those officials had overstepped their customary and legitimate authority.[67] In the coming months, the regulators would seek to keep pressure on government officials, while others, who sympathized with their goals if not their tactics, would continue to meet in county conventions. Meanwhile, Governor Bowdoin, the state legislature, and the Confederation Congress would attempt to devise a strategy to neutralize the threat of the people they called "mobs," "crowds," or "insurgents."

## 3 Mobilizing Authority and Resistance

SITUATED ON THE Connecticut River roughly five miles north of the Connecticut border and ninety miles west of Boston, the town of Springfield had been claimed as an English settlement a mere six years after the founding of Boston. Organized by Puritan migrant Samuel Pynchon as a place where Englishmen could engage in the fur trade with local Native Americans, Springfield began as the northernmost outpost of what became the Connecticut colony before the settlement was incorporated into Massachusetts Bay. Over the course of the eighteenth century, it became a market town where farmers could bring their surplus farm products for transport down the Connecticut River and into the larger Atlantic market. By the 1780s, Springfield was not only one of the largest towns in the western half of the state, but it was also the location of the U.S. federal arsenal. During the Revolutionary War, it had been chosen because of its central location within New England on a major river artery that was far enough inland to be safe from an attack by the British navy. In 1777 the Continental Congress leased ten acres from the town and constructed several buildings to store guns and ammunition and to cast artillery pieces. In the fall of 1786, the arsenal held more than seven thousand guns and bayonets, several hundred older guns, more than thirteen hundred barrels of gun powder, several cannon, and more than four hundred thousand pounds of ammunition.[1]

At the end of September 1786, the town was preparing for the county's quarterly session of the Supreme Judicial Court, which handled criminal cases. The court closures of the previous several weeks had all targeted the civil Court of Common Pleas, while a Supreme Judicial Court session had been conducted in Worcester in early September without any disruption. But in the days leading up to the Springfield session, Hampshire County sheriff Elisha Porter began to hear from informants that regulators were planning some action against the Supreme Judicial Court. The intelligence he received suggested that the insurgents would start to gather in town on Sunday night before the opening of the court session on Tuesday. To prevent them from gaining hold of the courthouse, Porter assembled a group of 40 volunteers who started guarding the courthouse on Saturday night. Meanwhile, the commander of the local militia, General William Shepard, was attempting to call out 200 militia members, but he was worried that he would not receive much support, for, as he told the governor, "from the coolness towards government which is too general & prevalent, the number and issue must be uncertain and precarious."[2] However, Porter's small defense force was joined by 150 men from neighboring Northampton and 50 more from the town of Hadley.[3]

On Monday, more militia members arrived ahead of the court officials, who made it to town that evening. It was unclear how many regulators planned to arrive, but Shepard received word that many had gathered in West Springfield directly across the Connecticut River; on Monday night he wrote to the governor that "I have just received intelligence that five hundred insurgents are to be embodied at west Springfield this evening and some say two thousand."[4] By Tuesday morning, September 26, the day the court session was scheduled to open, the number of militia who had come to Springfield reached approximately eight hundred. Several hundred of them arrived without guns, and Shepard decided that even though he did not have the legal authority to use weapons from the federal arsenal, he demanded that the keeper of the arsenal allow him to fully arm his men. In addition, Shepard also borrowed an artillery piece that was rolled down to the front door of the courthouse. As he later explained to Governor Bowdoin, Shepard thought it necessary to "demand and seize the key of the Arsenal and take from thence two hundred stands of arms."[5]

The eight hundred supporters of the court were opposed by upward of twelve hundred regulators, who gathered on Tuesday morning within sight of the militia forces. A majority of these insurgents arrived with guns, while others came with clubs. While significant numbers arrived from small towns throughout Hampshire County, Shepard believed that insurgents also came from Berkshire County to the west, Worcester to the east, and even the state of Connecticut to the south.[6]

As had been the case when the court was closed in Northampton the previous month, the town of Pelham sent a contingent of men to take part in the insurgency. This time, however, they were joined by Daniel Shays, a veteran of the Revolutionary War, who began his military service in 1775, eventually rose to the rank of captain, and remained in the army until October 1780, when he sought and received a discharge. Shays had declined to take part in the previous court closing in late August, but in Springfield he was seen as one of the leaders of the regulators.[7] By midday, with the militia in control of the courthouse and the armory, the crowd of regulators grew restless, and one eyewitness believed that "the Insurgents seemed determined to dispute the Ground" that was occupied by the militia forces. This led to a meeting between General Shepard and some of the leading insurgents, including Daniel Shays, and it was agreed the insurgents could march by the courthouse "provided that they would behave decently and offer no insult."[8] The militia forces arranged themselves on both sides of the street by the courthouse. As the "Insirgents marched thro' in good order,"[9] one eyewitness stated that "the disaffected militia had an opportunity of following their Inclination and joining the insurgents, as some did."[10] Most members of the militia, however, stood firm and did not switch sides to join the regulators. To distinguish themselves from each other, the militia forces put pieces of white paper in their hats, while the insurgents placed sprigs of evergreen or hemlock in theirs.[11]

At four o'clock that afternoon, the court session opened, but not enough potential jurors were there to empanel any juries, and by early Tuesday evening the court adjourned for the night. During the afternoon, the regulators formed a committee to draft a petition to send to the judges. These representatives included Rueben Dickinson (who had played a prominent role in the Ely uprising of 1782), Daniel Shays, and five other men. That evening, after the court had adjourned, the men brought the petition to the inn where the judges were spending the night, which happened to be in the midst of the regulator camp. In the petition, the regulators identified themselves as "the People collected now in Springfield in the County of Hampshire for the purpose of moderating government in said county." It informed the judges that the crowd did not want to prevent all of the court's activities but only those that might bring indictments against themselves or against the men who had closed the civil courts the previous month in Northampton. They also asked that the civil courts not meet again until "we can obtain Redress of Grievances" from the legislature.[12]

That evening, the men on both sides camped next to each other. Leaders established boundary lines, and guards were placed to prevent the two groups from provoking each other. As the eyewitness account in the *Hampshire Gazette* put it, "it looks a little more like the regular manoeuvers of an army: Both parties have their guards, and are regularly relieved, and no person can pass either, without a permit from their respective officers."[13] The next morning, the court procession, led by Sheriff Porter, walked through the regulator camp on its way to the courthouse. As it passed the insurgent guard, the procession received a "military Salute from them."[14] As the court session started, the insurgents asked the court to postpone its session until the meeting concluded, and the judges agreed to wait until midafternoon. The situation remained tense the rest of Wednesday, and while the justices did not give in to the demands of the insurgents, they were unable to empanel any grand juries. After another tense night, the court convened again on Thursday morning, but it was determined that the two cases that were prepared for trial should be postponed, "seeing the impracticability of a fair hearing amidst such confusion." The court then adjourned, and after another meeting between insurgent and militia leaders, the full militia force marched away from the courthouse back toward the armory. At that point, the eleven hundred or so insurgents "marched down by the Court House in marshall array."[15] According to General Shepard, another long discussion led to the following agreement: "We finally agreed by Committees of officers from each party that they should dismiss their men and give a signal, immediately after which I was to dismiss mine, and that all persons were to return home without injuring or insulting any person."[16]

## Protecting the Armory

One of the first people to receive news of the events in Springfield was Secretary of War Henry Knox, who happened to be in New York City consulting with members of the Confederation Congress. In the early 1770s, Knox had been a bookseller in Boston and a member of one of the militia companies that were growing increasingly restive under British occupation. After the battle of Lexington and Concord and the arrival of George Washington, Knox was able to befriend the commander, who came to recognize that Knox's book study of artillery technique made him a valuable addition to the Patriot ranks. Within a short time, Knox had become the Continental army's chief of artillery, and he served as a general during the Revolutionary War. Following the war, Knox concerned himself with managing the huge tracts of land he claimed in Maine, which had come into his possession thanks to his wife Lucy, whose father, Thomas Flucker, had fled along with other prominent loyalists during the American Revolution. In the immediate aftermath of the war, Knox had been instrumental in creating the Society of Cincinnati, a fraternal association of Revolutionary War officers that included most prominent generals, including George Washington. Many worried that the society would attempt to distinguish itself as a kind of American aristocracy, and its elaborate uniforms and decision to offer membership only to officers and their firstborn male descendants did not allay such fears.[17] Now, as secretary of war, Knox was responsible for protecting the government's store of weapons in Springfield. As it was, the armory sat exposed and undefended. In the fall of 1786, there were less than seven hundred soldiers in the entire U.S. armed force, and nearly all of them were stationed in forts in western Pennsylvania. Prior to the session of the Supreme Judicial Court, Knox had asked Bowdoin to provide troops to protect the armory, but Bowdoin had told him that since the armory and its contents were federal property, it was the responsibility of the Confederation Congress to provide such protection. In the meantime, Bowdoin had written General Shepard to tell him to do anything that Knox advised to protect the armory.

After hearing about the confrontation in Springfield, Knox left New York to visit Springfield and then Boston, and in early October he consulted with Bowdoin and an informal group of the governor's advisers, including Rufus King, who was one of Massachusetts's representatives in the Congress. Both Knox and Governor Bowdoin agreed that the armory was vulnerable, but they also recognized that neither the state nor the federal government had the money to raise additional troops to station in Springfield. In addition, there was a concern that if people in the Massachusetts countryside discovered plans to send federal troops to Springfield, it might alarm and possibly alienate them. As a result of these meetings, a plan was concocted to ask Congress to authorize troops for the armory without publicly announcing that the troops were needed there. Knox wrote to Congress to ask for eight hundred additional men, while providing them with reports that Native American groups in the Ohio Valley and elsewhere on the frontier were threatening war. Knox then followed up with a report on October 18 telling Congress that the troops were really needed to defend the armory against a possible takeover from armed insurgents: "It is my firm conviction unless the present commotions are checked with a strong hand, that an armed tyranny may be established on the ruins of the present constitution." He thought that there needed to be a guard of at least five hundred troops to protect the armory. However, he cautioned Congress that if it became public knowledge that the troops were going to protect the armory, there might be a powerful backlash in the Massachusetts countryside.[18]

In mid-October, Congress approved Knox's plan. It authorized an additional 1,340 new troops, nearly half from Massachusetts and the bulk of the rest from other New England states. Officially, the troops were being raised "on account of the hostile proceedings of several nations of the western Indians." But in a secret committee report, Congress acknowledged that "it appears that a dangerous insurrection has taken place in divers parts of the state of Massachusetts." The insurgents had already closed the courts in many counties, and it seemed clear that if the government did not take action to protect the armory, the insurgents "will possess themselves of the arsenal at Springfield, subvert the government, and not only reduce that commonwealth to a state of anarchy and confusion, but probably involve the United States in the calamities of a civil war." However, this secret committee report went on to say that "it is not expedient" to explain to the public that the troops were needed for that purpose.[19] To pay for the soldiers, the Congress's Board of Treasury recommended that $530,000 be requisitioned from the states, which would support $500,000 in loans paying 6 percent interest.

While Congress approved the plan, getting the states to raise troops and money proved exceptionally difficult. The Massachusetts legislature formally supported the measure, and Knox put Revolutionary War general Henry Jackson in charge of raising troops and soliciting loans from wealthy Bostonians. However, no state except Virginia approved of any funds to support the loan, and throughout the fall Jackson was essentially unable to convince anyone in Boston either to loan the government money to support the troops or to sign up to serve in such a force. After nearly two months of trying, Jackson had signed up only eighty recruits. It is true that one group that did express interest in supporting the militia was rejected. In late November, Governor Bowdoin received a letter from Prince Hall, an African American resident of Boston who had been instrumental in the founding of a fraternal organization called the "African Lodge of Free Masons." Hall pledged that African American men who belonged to the Lodge were willing to join the militia to help end the insurgency, but Governor Bowdoin ignored his offer.[20]

Meanwhile, many in Massachusetts believed that the official reason given for raising the troops—that is, to put down a possible Indian uprising—was nothing more than a lie. Rufus King received a letter from fellow congressional representative Elbridge Gerry who reported that some representatives in the state legislature saw through the ruse: "Some of the country members laugh and say the Indian War is only a political one to obtain a standing army."[21] Colonel James Swan wrote to Knox to tell him slyly that "I hope in this declaration 'Indians,'—is meant all those who oppose the Dignity, honour, and happiness of the United States."[22]

In the fall of 1786, Massachusetts was not the only state where rural protest was taking place. For example, in neighboring New Hampshire, anger at a legislature that refused to support paper money and other relief measures prompted a few hundred farmers to assemble in the town of Kingston on September 20 and march several miles east to Exeter, where the state legislature was in session. The crowd surrounded the meetinghouse where the legislature sat and declared that it would not leave until its petitions were addressed. The governor, General John Sullivan, ignored the crowd's demands, and the legislature continued to meet. That evening, as night began to fall, a group of leaders in Exeter charged toward the crowd, which was forced to disperse to a camp about a mile away. Governor Sullivan called out the militia from eastern towns, which went after the insurgents the next day, overran the camp, and arrested thirty-nine men. They were brought back to Exeter, where they were forced to parade with their hats off while they were jeered by the crowd. Facing charges of treason, the leaders of the crowd were willing to make confessions of their wrongdoing, and most were released after confirming their loyalty to the state.[23]

## Responding to the Regulation

As these events unfolded, the Massachusetts legislature prepared to meet to respond to the convention movement and the wave of court closures. On September 13, Governor Bowdoin had recalled the legislature, and on September 28 both houses settled into their seats to hear the governor's opening address. He cautioned that the disturbances of the previous month threatened the independent and representative government that had been so costly and difficult to forge. For Bowdoin, many of the current disturbances were the result of "wicked and artful men," who were convincing people either to oppose the government or to not get involved to actively protect it. If such men were allowed to operate, they would continue to weaken and ultimately "destroy all confidence in Government." For Bowdoin, it was a "moral certainty" that the legislature would address any actual grievances, because if a law happened to get passed that produced any harmful effects, those effects would also be felt by the legislators themselves.[24] Bowdoin told the legislators that they would try to understand the reasons why people had decided to use force to close the courts, so that they could prevent similar problems in the future. However, he argued that no matter what the causes were, the disturbances themselves could never be justified. Any grievances felt by the people of Massachusetts had to be addressed by the state legislature, and any efforts to organize relief through any other group—for example, a county convention—was "anticonstitutional, & of very dangerous tendency, even when attempted in a peaceable manner."[25] The efforts of the people had to be directed to actively support the operation of government, and not by calling its actions into question. The governor then directed the legislature to "take the most vigorous measures . . . to vindicate the insulted dignity of Government" and ensure that the laws were respected.[26]

While Bowdoin was making his address to the legislature in Boston, representatives from forty-one towns in Worcester County were meeting in the town of Paxton. They wrote to the legislature that they represented "the collective voice of the county," and they wanted relief from a variety of grievances, especially the twin problems of private and public debt. Debt and taxes were so high, and the money supply was so low, that forced property sales would only serve to impoverish the people: "The produce of the present year, and the remainder of our cattle, even were we to sell the whole, are totally inadequate to the present demands for money." As it was, "an amazing flood of lawsuits" had resulted in "many industrious members of the community" being forced into jail. Like previous conventions, this meeting in Worcester County not only addressed the government but also appealed to the people directly. Convention members believed that their efforts were supported by the spirit of the Constitution, which they said should operate "for the protection, safety, prosperity and happiness of the people; and not for the honour or interest of any man, family, or class of men."[27]

The legislature not only received petitions from Worcester County but also heard from two other county conventions and at least ten towns. The problems identified in these petitions were similar to the issues raised by the summer county conventions. For example, the first petition received during this session of the legislature was from the town of Dracut in northern Middlesex County. Again, the question of the money supply figured prominently: the lack of currency meant that the prices that townspeople could receive for farm products or their own property were very low. The petition openly wondered where the money had gone, suggesting that it had been sent to a foreign country, or it had "hid itself in the secret Confines of those who have a greater love to their own Interest then they have to that of their Neighbours." Without some drastic action, the people of Dracut said it would be impossible "to Extricate themselves from the Labyrinth of Debt into which they are fallen." As it was, "Individuals are Constantly hauled away" to jail because they were unable to pay their debts.[28]

Reform of the legal system was also a priority of Dracut and other towns. Dracut asked for legislation that would allow debtors to pay their debts with property assessed by people and the town and not auctioned off for whatever it might fetch. Dracut and other towns were also influenced by a series of essays that appeared in state newspapers in the spring of 1786 under the name Honestus. These essays were very critical of lawyers who collected high legal fees from already impoverished and burdened debtors. At one point, Honestus even called for the abolition of the legal profession in the state.[29] Dracut also bemoaned the high costs of the legal system, and petitioned for an abolition of the Court of Common Pleas, and it supported the idea of moving the state capital out of Boston. In addition to the relative expense of the city, the town worried that wealthy and well-connected city residents had much greater access to channels of political power: "Because considering the depravity of human Nature, & how liable Men are to be Biased, the number & Abilities of ye Inhabitants of that town, and the Opportunity they have to converse with the members of the General Court, we think throws more than a Proportionable weight into the Scale of Legislation in their Favour."[30]

Many other towns echoed the call for reduced tax burdens, court reform, and relocation of the capital. A few were quite strident in tone. The town of Plympton in Bristol County threatened that "the Government immediately over us is become very Burdensome so that the People can not subsist under it very much longer but they will rise in open Rebelion."[31] Other petitions—especially those from the selectmen of Groton and Rowley—were more supportive of the government, but they also recognized the sense of desperation felt by many. In Groton, selectmen like Oliver Prescott had been facing outspoken defiance from many prominent members of their town, especially Job Shattuck, who had played a prominent role in the closing of the Middlesex County court in Concord back in September. The petition from the selectmen went to great pains to criticize the efforts of Shattuck and others, whom they viewed "with utter abhorrence." They believed that the closing of the court was illegal and had been fomented "by the insinuation & misrepresentations of a few wicked and designing men, full frought with Ambition, Envy & Ignorance." However, although the selectmen believed that there were untrustworthy and devious men trying to stir up trouble, the fact remained that many people in the countryside were in a difficult economic situation, and the selectmen were cognizant of "the general uneasiness which pervades this Commonwealth." They believed that the people just did not have the ability to pay the taxes that had been levied, and aggressive collection of outstanding taxes would fail to provide the income that the state expected. According to Prescott and the other selectmen, "the greater part of the common people" were in possession of land, but many "have parted with their personal Estates, and are reduced to one or two cows only."[32]

While hearing from towns and counties, the legislature was also made aware of disturbances that continued in the countryside. In early October, the Supreme Judicial Court was scheduled to sit in Great Barrington in Berkshire County, but in the immediate aftermath of Springfield the Berkshire judges decided to postpone the session before it started. Nonetheless, between 150 and 200 insurgents took possession of the courthouse. Acting unopposed, at least some insurgents did some minor damage to the courthouse building, one man cursed and waved a gun, and another attempted to rob homes in the vicinity.[33] A week later, during the night of October 10, a handful of insurgents from Plymouth County snuck onto the fort on Dorchester neck—which in the eighteenth century connected the peninsula of Boston to the rest of the mainland—and attempted to make off with the cannon of the fort. The men were discovered and were unable to steal the cannon, but this action so close to Boston added to the tension.[34] Later in October, fewer than 100 insurgents attempted to disrupt a Bristol County court in Taunton, but again militia commander David Cobb had taken preemptive action by calling out supporters ahead of time and placing a cannon at the front door of the courthouse. Roughly 375 militiamen gathered near the courthouse before any regulators arrived, and so the crowd could only present a petition to the court.[35]

At the end of October, the governor decided to call for a vigorous militia presence to ensure that the court in Cambridge across the Charles River from Boston could operate unimpeded. Government supporters from Boston, Cambridge, and other nearby towns marched, so that when the court opened there were more than two thousand militia members present. In the more commercially oriented eastern counties like Essex and Suffolk, few residents offered support for paper money and other debtor-relief measures. This was certainly true for wealthy creditors themselves, but it was also true for many urban artisans and even laborers, whose livelihoods were dependent on distant markets, and who believed that paper money and other pro-debtor legislation would only hurt such economic activity. No regulators appeared at this session of the court, and it took place without incident.[36]

Over the course of the next several weeks, the legislature did pass some relief measures to aid both taxpayers and debtors. First, taxpayers were allowed to pay previous specie taxes in a variety of farm products, including beef, pork, grains, cloth, or lumber. Artisans could pay in leather, nails, cedar shingles, and other such products, while taxpayers in coastal towns could submit fish or whale oil in order to pay their tax bill.[37] The legislature also extended the deadline for the most recent tax from January 1 to April 31, 1787.[38] Other tax measures included an agreement to try to raise money through sale of government lands in Maine, and a new tax on imported luxury items like silver, jewelry, and china.[39] Finally, the legislature agreed to a demand voiced back in the summer to redirect one-third of the impost and excise taxes away from payments to creditors and toward the government treasury.

In addition to efforts to alleviate some of the tax burden, the legislature also made minor efforts to reduce the expenses of the legal system. An act of November 15 allowed debt cases where the total debt was four pounds or less to be handled by a justice of the peace, which could save several court fees that were associated with the court of common pleas.[40] The legislature also passed a relief law for debtors. For a period of eight months, debtors would not be required to either pay in specie or have property auctioned off. Instead, if the creditor wanted to collect, the debtor's property would be appraised by three impartial evaluators to determine the value of the property, and the creditor would have to accept that property in lieu of cash. However, this law allowed the creditor—and not the debtor—to choose which property was to be appraised and turned over, and it still authorized the jailing of debtors if they did not have enough property to pay their debts.[41]

While the legislature did enact some modest reforms, it rejected the most fundamental demands of the regulators and county conventions. The legislature voted against a bill for an emission of paper money, and it refused to entertain the closure of the courts until the following election. It referred the request to have the capital moved to a legislative committee. In addition, the legislature was also intent on trying to prevent further disturbances at court sessions. It passed legislation to prevent those called to militia service from refusing to serve or supporting the insurgency by reorganizing the state militia and spelling out harsh penalties for soldiers who refused their orders and deserted: "Whatsosever Officer or soldier shall abandon any post committed to his charge, or shall speak words inducing others to do the like in time of an engagement, shall suffer death."[42] Four days later, the legislature passed a Riot Act, which empowered sheriffs, constables, and justices of the peace to read a proclamation before any group that threatened to use violence. The proclamation would warn those assembled that they had one hour to peacefully disperse, and if they refused to do so, they could be arrested and potentially face the loss of property ("all their lands, tenements, goods, and chattels"), six months to a year in jail, and physical punishment of "thirty nine stripes on the naked back, at the Public whipping-post." The Riot Act also specified lesser punishments for those bystanders who refused to aid officers in the arrest of rioters, and it also declared that if officials happened to injure or kill any rioters who resisted arrest, they could not be charged with a crime themselves.[43]

As the legislature worked, the governor made it aware of ongoing insurgent activity in Hampshire County. He pointed to a circular letter that originated in the town of Pelham and was addressed to the selectmen of other towns in the county. The letter, which would be reproduced in the *Hampshire Gazette*, warned citizens that the government was "determined to call all those who appeared to stop the Court to condign punishment." In other words, there was a belief that the government was planning to arrest, try, and execute those who had taken part in earlier court closings. Recalling the organization that had taken place in the countryside back in 1774 and 1775, the letter called for towns to organize and be ready to respond in a moment's notice: "Therefore I request you to assemble your men together, to see that they are well armed and equipped with sixty rounds each man, and to be ready to turn out at a minute's warning; likewise to be properly organized with officers." The letter was signed by Daniel Shays. While the regulator letter appeared to be calling people to arm themselves to defend against a government incursion, Governor Bowdoin saw it as a sign of a regulator offensive. It was, therefore, "very dangerous to the peace & safety of the Commonwealth."[44]

Three days after the legislature was made aware of this apparent military organization in Hampshire County, it decided to suspend the Writ of Habeas Corpus. According to the language of the legislation, recently "armed bodies of men" had engaged in "violent and outrageous opposition" to the state's authority. Therefore, Governor Bowdoin and his council were empowered to authorize the arrest of anyone "whom the Governor and Council shall deem the safety of the Commonwealth requires should be restrained of their personal liberty." If the governor issued a warrant for the arrest of anyone, the local sheriff or other official had "full power forceably to enter any Dwelling House or any other Building, in which they shall have reason to suspect any person, required by such Warrant to be apprehended is concealed." These persons could be held without bail until July of 1787.[45]

The final major piece of legislation was an effort to convince regulators to abandon their activity with a promise that they would not be prosecuted if they agreed to give up their arms and take an oath of allegiance to government. According to the legislation, which passed on November 15, "many deluded persons . . . have forcibly interrupted the regular administration of

Law and Justice" and had "committed outrages which tend to the utter sub-
version of the Constitutional authority thereof." The legislature was willing
to forgive such actions taken between June and the date the legislation, if
the person in question took an oath of allegiance by January 1, 1787, and engaged in no more similar behavior. Anyone who failed to take the Oath of
Allegiance "shall be subject to be apprehended and tried before the Justices
of the Supreme Judicial Court," either in the county in which the offenses
took place or "in any County within this Commonwealth nearest thereto,
where Law and Justice can be administered without apprehension of inter-
ruption."[46]

Along with passing the indemnity act, the legislature tried to summa-
rize, clarify, and defend its actions by issuing "An Address . . . to the People
of the Commonwealth" on November 14. While the legislature recognized
that there were many important concerns that needed to be addressed, they
agreed with Governor Bowdoin that much of the conflict was the result of
"evil & designing men" hoping "to alienate the affections of the people,"
and the legislature believed that much of the opposition to government was
based on "misinformation." In an attempt to stop such misinformation, the
legislature provided details on the cost of government, the scope of the state
debt, and the amount of recent tax levies. After acknowledging that not everyone would agree with their efforts, they reminded the people of Massachusetts of an obvious point: "It never can be the case, that the whole community shall be of the same opinion." The legislature said that the rule of the
majority must be maintained: "Unless we submit to be controuled by the
greater number, the Commonwealth must break into pieces;—but neither
will the inhabitants of any County or Town be all of the same sentiment, each
man therefore must be a part, and the whole reduced to a state of nature." It
also acknowledged that some people wanted a revision of the state constitution but that such a revision would likely be very complicated and time-
consuming. The legislature's address went into detail to explain why it was
unwilling to approve paper money legislation. It rejected paper money because it believed that the only people who would benefit from such a system
would be the "artfull & unprincipled," while those who would suffer would
be "the Widow & the orphan; the simple and unwary; the most innocent &
defenceless part of the Community." The legislature was convinced that the
currency shortfall was the direct result of "Habits of Luxury" which led people to buy unnecessary "Gewgaws imported from Europe, & the more perni-

cious Produce of the West Indies." Therefore, the solution advocated by the legislature was identical to the one offered by Governor Bowdoin: if people were more self-disciplined and avoided such luxuries, they would not need the quick fix of paper currency.[47]

To conclude the appeal, the legislature warned the people that it was not going to allow a situation in which "a Spirit of unreasonable Jealousy & a complaining Temper are indulged." Recalling the Old Testament story in which the Israelites complained to God and "wantonly provoked his anger," the legislature warned its audience that Massachusetts might be headed to a similar fate, in which the people rebuked God "with Murmuring & Ingratitude & provoke him to destroy us." According to the legislature, "When the People are dissatisfied with the Conduct of any Government, it may at least deserve a Reflection, whether the Difficulty is not with themselves." To save themselves, the legislators implored local ministers to inculcate "the Principles of Justice and publick Virtue." They addressed officers to serve as examples as well as enforcers of the law to prevent future disturbances. And they also directly addressed those who had remained on the sidelines. These "inactive Spectators" were like the man who stood idly by watching his own house burn, at peace with the fact that "he did not set it on fire." They concluded their address by stating that the only ones who might continue intimidating the courts were "deaf to the Voice of Reason, and lost to all Sense of Justice and Virtue." They were warned that while "Considerations of Friendship and Affinity may delay the Time of Recompense," it would not prevent the "Vengance of an injured Community" from engaging in vigorous punishment.[48]

**Conflict from Springfield to Petersham**

AFTER PASSING THE relief legislation, including the act of indemnity, and issuing the appeal to the public, the legislature ended its fall session on November 18, 1786. Word of the indemnity offer and copies of the appeal would take days or weeks to reach people throughout the state. Meanwhile, a court session was scheduled for Worcester on November 21. To prevent the court from sitting, dozens of insurgents arrived from Shrewsbury, Hubbardstown, and other neighboring towns. Led by Abraham Gale of the town of Princeton, Massachusetts, the insurgents seized the courthouse. The judges convened the next day at nearby Patch's tavern, where they received a petition from the insurgents to adjourn until after the next election. The judges refused, and they proceeded from the tavern to the courthouse, led by the county sheriff, William Greenleaf. The court procession "walked through the ranks of the insurgents, who had opened to the right and left, but were stopped a little distance from the steps by three rows of pointed bayonets." Sheriff Greenleaf then read the Riot Act to the assembled regulators, but without any militia support, he had no allies and was unable to take any steps to arrest the assembled men.[1]

The next session of the Court of Common Pleas was scheduled to meet in

Cambridge on November 28. Regulators from Worcester County, including Adam Wheeler and Abraham Gale, met with Job Shattuck from Groton, who had played a prominent role in closing the Middlesex County court in Concord back in September. Shattuck had been in communication with fellow Groton resident and supporter of government Oliver Prescott, and those two men were working on an agreement where the regulators would not march as long as the militia was not called out.[2] When the Worcester insurgents realized that Shattuck was considering not taking part in the court closing, they apparently put pressure on him to encourage him to participate. The efforts from Worcester leaders led Shattuck to change his mind, and he agreed to lead Groton-area regulators toward Cambridge. Meanwhile, word arrived that no regulators would be coming from Bristol County, because most of them believed that the reforms passed by the state legislature made armed protest no longer necessary.[3] Meanwhile, regulators in Hampshire County were also organizing and moving into Worcester County but did not catch up with their counterparts further east. About three hundred of them made it as far east as Shrewsbury in eastern Worcester County, where they sent a scout ahead.[4]

As regulator leaders made their plans for Cambridge, Governor Bowdoin was making his own. He had received the word that the Worcester court had been forced to close, and he was receiving information that insurgents were planning to attempt the same in Cambridge. Bowdoin decided that he needed to make a very strong show of support for government, and he called for militia commanders in Suffolk, Middlesex, and Essex counties to send troops. As a force of two thousand or more militia troops made its way into Cambridge, the groups of regulators recognized that they would be outnumbered, and those who had been preparing to converge on the court decided not to show up. Among them was Job Shattuck, who led his band of regulators from the towns surrounding Groton as far as Concord before deciding to return home.

Meanwhile, Groton selectman Oliver Prescott had written the governor to identify Shattuck and others as men who played a prominent role in the regulation. On November 28, he sent word that Shattuck, Oliver Parker, Benjamin Page, Nathan Smith, and John Kelsey "have been active in the late rebellion & stirring up the people to oppose government, are therefore dangerous persons & May a Warrant may be issued to restrain them of their personal Liberty."[5] Governor Bowdoin agreed, and he authorized a cavalry force of three hundred from Cambridge and surrounding towns to find and arrest the five men. The men on horseback, led by Boston lawyer Benjamin Hitchborn, "consisted of lawyers, physicians and merchants [who] were joined by a number of Gentlemen from the county as they passed through it."[6] The men were able to capture Oliver Parker and Benjamin Page in Concord, but Shattuck managed to escape back toward his Groton home, with militia leaders on horseback in pursuit. In possession of the arrest warrant signed by the governor, the party burst in Shattuck's house, where it encountered his wife and several children, but not Shattuck himself. The men then rode to a neighbor's house, where they discovered that he had recently left. They followed tracks in the fresh snow and caught up to Shattuck as he was walking back toward his house around ten o'clock the next morning. One member of the government's party jumped on Shattuck, and the two fell, and rolled down the hill near the banks of the Nashua River.[7] Shattuck was armed with a sword, which he unsheathed as the two men struggled. Other members of the government party joined in the effort to subdue Shattuck, and in the struggle Shattuck was struck by a sword, which opened a large wound above his right knee. Fearing that nearby regulators might try to free Shattuck and the others from jail, the government party was directed to bring him and the others to jail in Boston. In the immediate vicinity, news of Shattuck's capture led to some retaliation. A constable who had aided in Shattuck's arrest had his property set on fire, while a local lawyer was threatened with having his law office burned down.[8]

Word of the capture of Job Shattuck and the others quickly spread through the countryside, and as the story traveled, it became more and more dramatic. Rumors began to spread that Shattuck had been killed and that members of his family, including women and children, had been stabbed or sliced with swords. When Bowdoin heard that other prominent insurgents were in Shrewsbury, he sent another cavalry force armed with arrest warrants for regulators Adam Wheeler and Abraham Gale from Worcester County. It were unable to find Wheeler or Gale, but tavern keeper Thomas Farmer was "abused and threatend in his house with pistols," and another bystander was wounded on the hand.[9] These attacks by forces loyal to government seemed to confirm some of the worst fears of the regulators, and following the attacks, it is likely that they redoubled their efforts to encourage others to join them in the movement. A copy of a letter dated December 2 and carried by regulator Sylvanius Billings alluded to the government attacks and the capture of Job Shattuck and others and encouraged people to join "we that Stile ourselves Rigelators" in order to challenge a government that was threatening the rights of the people "as this is perelous times and blood Shed and prisoners made." According to the letter, the government was composed of "tirants who are fighting for promotion and to advance their Intrest wich will Destroy the good people of this Land." If such men were not opposed, they would pose a threat to people throughout the commonwealth. Therefore, the regulators believed that "it is our Duty to stand for our lives and for our familys and for our Intrest wich will be taken from us if we Dont Defend them." In letters and by word of mouth, such appeals were broadcast across the interior of the state, as the regulators hoped that people would "fly to our assistance as Soon as posable in this just and righteous cause."[10]

In some towns, especially in parts of northern Worcester and Hampshire counties, the call for greater participation in the regulator movement was widely supported. Towns such as Colrain, Whatley, Pelham, and Hubbardstown overwhelmingly supported the regulator cause, while other towns supported the government, were divided, or preferred to remain on the sidelines. While a town's location and economy certainly influenced local opinion, allegiances were forged in the crucible of local communities, as family, friends, and neighbors met in taverns, after church, and in town meetings to discuss and debate the proper course of action. And while inhabitants in some towns had been paying close attention to the growing conflict, those in many other towns were less aware of the controversies. Some found themselves pulled into the conflict by early December. For example, the town of Rowe in the northwest corner of the state wrote an open letter claiming that its residents had been "repeatedly requested to join in the dispute between the government and those called the Regulating party." Unable to discover "the true cause of the dispute which renders it impossible for us to determine what is best to be done," the people were not sure what to do. The town decided that those who were able to leave town would "march . . . to that place that they can obtain the best information of the true state of affairs and (if need be) join the party they shall judge to be in the right."[11]

Following the capture of Shattuck and the government foray into Shrewsbury, the next court session was scheduled for Worcester on December 5. While the regulators were attempting to recruit and organize more support, Worcester County militia commander Jonathan Warner was aware of the regulator activity, and he labored to ensure that militiamen would come to

Worcester to defend the court. He told local militia officers to round up men and bring them to Worcester with three days' worth of provisions. He told the governor that in some towns, including Brookfield, he received a positive response, but men in other towns were reluctant or unwilling to turn out. Warner told the governor that if he wanted to ensure protection of the Worcester court, he would need to send "a formidable force" from Boston and the surrounding towns, "and Perhaps some Pieces of artillery."[12] On Sunday night, December 3, regulators began to arrive in Worcester, and they seized control of the courthouse. The next morning, a call for militia brought about 170 supporters of government out as well. These militia marched past the assembled regulators at the courthouse and on to a local tavern. Tensions increased when rumors spread that a cavalry unit was approaching from Boston. While such rumors proved false, the regulators remained on high alert.

In the communities surrounding Worcester, both regulators and militia made preparations to march into town for the court session scheduled for the next day. That evening, however, a "violent snow storm" began. The *Worcester Magazine* stated that it was the worst storm in recent memory, which made travel from neighboring communities nearly impossible. The next morning, the snow continued "with redoubled fury," and that prevented more militia from arriving from county towns like Leominster and Brookfield. However, some insurgents from Holden and other towns did make it to Worcester. The storm prevented at least one judge from arriving, but the justices did open the court session at the Sun tavern in town and then proceeded to adjourn the court until January 23.[13] More regulators started to arrive the next day, including Daniel Shays, who arrived with a force estimated to be nearly 350. By this point, the number of regulators in town had grown to between 800 and 1,000 men. The men pressured local residents in order to seek shelter from the storm, but they did not force their way into homes where they were refused. At least one of the judges, Artemas Ward of Shrewsbury, had remained in town, and the insurgents presented him with petitions from the county towns of Sutton and Douglas, which asked that the court be postponed until spring.[14]

Most of the men left town on Thursday, but not before submitting another petition to Ward. According to the *Worcester Magazine*, the regulator leaders had met with prominent members of the county convention. The petition they crafted was sent from a committee representing several towns in Worcester, and from "a BODY of MEN" from Worcester, Hampshire, and Berkshire counties. They wanted to make it clear that their complaints were not coming from a "factious few" but were instead the concerns shared by "almost every individual who derives his living from the labour of his hands or an income of a farm." While they "greatfully acknowledge" the efforts that the legislature made to address some of their grievances, they were far from satisfied. First, they expressed "horrour" that the government had suspended the writ of habeas corpus. They believed that doing so was "dangerous, if not absolutely destructive to a Republican Government." Since the passage of that legislation, Job Shattuck and others had been whisked away to a jail far from home, and were "now languishing (if alive) under their wounds." The petitioners then repeated the rumors that had been heard throughout the countryside: "Your Petitioners have been informed that the eyes and breasts of women and children have been wounded, if not destroyed." The petitioners then reminded the governor and legislature of their struggles to defend their customary rights from British encroachment: "In vindication of our liberties, your Petitioners beg leave to point to your Excellency and your Honours the arguments used by our virtuous asserters of liberty against the act of British Parliament, in conveying our countrymen from county to county, and even beyond the sea for trial." The petitioners demanded a new act of indemnity, and a suspension of the courts in Worcester, Hampshire, and Berkshire counties until after the next election.[15]

In addition to making these demands, the petitioners attempted to show government officials how committed they were to their cause. They stated that they were not worried about their own safety; they were not motivated to petition by the "Mean fear of Death." They believed that "one moment of liberty to be worth an eternity of bondage." They recalled their experiences in the recent war for Independence by claiming that they also did not fear "the uncertainty of war, the injuries of hunger, cold, nakedness, or the infamous name of rebel." All of those things had been faced during the American Revolution, and the men had emerged victorious. Rather than more direct action, they continued to petition because of their "love to the people, and a horrour of the thoughts of the cruelties and devastation of a civil war."[16]

The weather remained extremely cold on Thursday, December 7, as the regulators began to disperse. Many returned to their homes, while others joined Daniel Shays in Rutland, where a barracks had been built during the Revolutionary War to house British soldiers captured at the battle of Saratoga. Still others remained in Worcester until Saturday, when another snowstorm hit "with almost incredible fury."[17] On December 9, regulators in Hampshire County organized themselves into six regiments led by a "Committee of Seventeen." Each regiment had two or three captains from towns in the county whose responsibility it was to organize and lead the various companies and regiments. There was a chairman of the committee, but each of the leaders was given the rank of captain and was charged with trying to raise troops in his town and then "Organising the regiments agreeable to martial order."[18] For example, the fourth regiment was to be led by Captain Daniel Shays of Pelham, Captain Hines of Greenwich, and Captain Billings of Amherst. The regulator captains sought to find soldiers who would serve in their units and apparently even had them sign enlistment papers: "We do each of us acknowledge our Selves to be Inlisted into a Company . . . in Col. Hazelton's Regement of Regulators in Order for the Suppressing of tyrannical governmint in the Massachusetts State." Soldiers signed up for a three-month term (at forty shillings per month) and agreed to "Ingage to abay Such Orders as we Shal Receive from time to time from Our Superer officers."[19]

In the weeks that followed, Governor Bowdoin sought and received intelligence on the regulators and advice about what to do next. Some observers suggested that the regulators were not an immediate threat. For example, two Boston lawyers who traveled through the countryside in early December wrote to the governor to tell him that they believed that the regulators would disband if Shattuck and the other state prisoners were released, and the courts were suspended until after the next elections.[20] However, most of the men writing the governor in December 1786 believed that the time for concessions had passed, and decisive military action was needed to end the insurgency. One of the challenges for the government would be raising (and paying for) a loyal militia that was large enough to overpower the regulator force. While the state militia forces had proved to be fairly reliable in the communities surrounding Boston, it was not entirely clear how robust the turnout would be in the state's interior, especially between Worcester and Berkshire counties. Meanwhile, General Henry Jackson had raised fewer than one hundred men to serve in the force authorized by the Confederation Congress. In addition, tax collection had essentially ceased in many parts of the state since the court closings began in August, and Bowdoin simply had no money in the treasury to equip and pay any troops who might be called out.[21] An additional consideration for Bowdoin was a recognition that any force raised by the government should be large enough to decisively defeat

thinking that another example of regulator intimidation might goad more people into actively supporting the government, or perhaps believing that the bitterly cold winter weather would keep the regulators away. About three hundred armed regulators arrived ahead of the justices, and they presented a petition to adjourn the session. The next day, after discussion between the judges and regulator representatives Luke Day, Thomas Grover, and Daniel Shays, the judges agreed.[26] An eyewitness account from government supporter Levi Shepard of Northampton described the three leaders and noted that Daniel Shays "is very thoughtfull, and appears like a man crouded with embarrassments, but the other leaders are very insolent & imperious."[27] Levi Shepard worried that the lack of a government presence in Springfield was giving the regulators more confidence: "They now exult on their return and plume themselves that government is now yielding to their demands so fast that Shays informed his men when he dismissed them that he was in hopes that he should not find it necessary to call them out any more on the like occasion."[28] Shepard was also upset that the justices of the court had allowed two of the regulators, Thomas Grover and Luke Day, to sit at their table and have a meal with them as they presented their petition.[29] Shepard was of the mind that men who intimidated the judges in order to stop the courts did not merit that kind of recognition or respect.

Another witness and government supporter, William Lyman, was outraged that the court had to agree to "the illegal & unjust demands of a pack of villains," and although the government had lost that particular battle, Lyman was optimistic that the government forces would soon win the war: "The leaders of the insurgents appear dejected and melancholy since their fruitless expedition to the eastward. They are under fearful apprehensions of being taken & lodged with their friends, Shattuck, Parker & Page. It is of great importance that government exerts itself immediately, I think their leaders can be taken better now than ever."[30] When the agreement had been reached, one of the judges who had been forced to sign the agreement noted that the regulators began to disperse, and "No injuries or insults were offered to individuals."[31] All three of these eyewitness accounts suggest that the aims of the regulators remained limited and focused. Despite the organization that was taking place in Hampshire County, and despite having a force of more than three hundred armed men within sight of the essentially undefended Springfield armory, the regulators did not make any attempt to seize weapons or ammunition.

## Mobilizing for Conflict

Five days before the regulators came to Springfield to close the court, Governor Bowdoin had begun two weeks of meetings with the Governor's Council.[32] On the basis of the intelligence and advice received by Ward, Shepard, and others, the governor and his councilors crafted a plan that would call for a militia force from eastern counties to be joined by a Worcester militia, as well as a force from Hampshire County under William Shepard. The militia force would bring arrest warrants for the leading insurgents, signed by the governor, to be given to the county sheriffs, and the militia would aid in the capture of the wanted men. The entire militia force was to be commanded by Benjamin Lincoln, the Revolutionary War general from the coastal town of Hingham who during the Revolutionary War had been forced to surrender the port of Charles Town in South Carolina but had later accepted Lord Cornwallis's sword following the American victory at Yorktown. After serving for a time as secretary of war for the Confederation Congress, Lincoln returned to Hingham in an effort to manage significant land claims in Maine. As the state's most prominent Revolutionary War veteran, Lincoln was seen as the most suitable man to lead the force against the regulators.[33]

After the conclusion of these meetings on January 4, Bowdoin authorized a total force of 4,400 soldiers: 2,000 from the counties immediately surrounding Boston, 1,200 from Worcester, and 1,200 from Hampshire County. The troops were to be paid by the towns from which they came, but General Lincoln estimated that £6,000 would be required to pay for one month of supplies for the troops. Because the legislature was not yet back in session, the governor would need to directly solicit an emergency loan from wealthy Bostonians. However, following the call for troops, the loan pledges only trickled in, even with the governor himself personally pledging £250. As Benjamin Lincoln related to George Washington, he decided to make a direct appeal to leading town merchants by meeting personally with a group of them and telling them it made sense for them to sacrifice some of their wealth in order to ensure the survival of the rest. Lincoln's appeal to the elite of Boston succeeded where Henry Jackson's had failed, and he was able to convince 130 men to pledge a total of £5,021, ranging in sums from £3 to £300.[34]

In addition to securing the funds necessary to supply the armed force, the government needed to ensure that enough men would answer the call to join the militia. On January 12, Governor Bowdoin issued "An Address to the Good People of the Commonwealth," in which he implored the citizens of the commonwealth to volunteer. Bowdoin said that back on October 24, the legislature gave him the authority to do whatever was necessary to restore order in the state. Despite the efforts of the legislature to address the concerns of the people, there continued to be disturbances that closed the courts in Hampshire and Worcester counties. Therefore, the governor had to use the authority granted him by the legislature to authorize a state militia force to assemble. That force would protect the courts in Worcester, stop the insurgents, and capture "all disturbers of the public peace." Bowdoin believed that the actions of the insurgents proved that they were determined "to annihilate our present happy constitution" or make the legislature pass laws "repugnant to every idea of justice, good faith, and national policy." In order to protect the government, Bowdoin called on "men of principle, the friends of justice and the Constitution," to stand up to protect their government. Those who failed to do so would be an "accessory to . . . their country's ruin." Bowdoin was hoping for the formation of a very large force that would prevent the need for bloodshed.[35]

Even before Bowdoin and his council began to meet, some towns in Worcester County began to petition for the release of Job Shattuck and the other prisoners held in Boston. One such petition dated December 19 was sent from the town of Ashburnham in Worcester County. The members of the town told the governor that no one in the town had gone to the last county convention or had played any role in stopping the county courts. They believed that such actions threatened to "disturb our peace, [and] weaken our Excellent Constitution." However, despite their support of government up to this point, residents of the town were very concerned about the recent government arrests and incursions in the countryside, "which we think has a direct tendency, to inflaim the minds of the people, against the officers of Government." They wanted the courts closed until the next election, those captured set free, and an assurance that no one who was "a peaceable Subject" would be arrested or "molested in person or property."[36] Another petition, dated January 1, 1787, came from the town of New Braintree and hoped to persuade the government that its view of the regulators was incorrect: such men were not simply poor and dispossessed men trying to upset the social order but were instead "a large number of the calm, steady & sensible yeomanry, men of good principals and large property."[37] Two days later, a petition was sent from the people of Winchendon, who pleaded with the government not to try to use force to put down the insurgency. "It will not do to settle these matters by fire & sword," they declared, but rather "for the parties to unite in a peaceable way & maner."[38]

Without doubt, many towns struggled to reach a consensus on an issue that forced most to take a side. Several weeks after the Winchendon petition was sent, the government received another petition from the selectmen of that town, who said that only about half of the town attended the previous meeting that had crafted the first petition. It was their belief that about one-third of the town was opposed to the petition, and "all the Selectmen together with Abel Wilder Esq. and a number of others who are men of Interest did all that was in their power to prevent the Town from Petitioning in the manner they did as we knew not what crime those persons mentioned in the Petition were guilty of."[39] A similar conflict emerged in the town of Brookfield, which responded to a call from regulators in December to petition the legislature for the continued closure of the courts, the reinstatement of habeas corpus, and a new indemnity act for those who had closed the courts in late November and December. This petition from the town as a whole, dated January 1, was followed by another petition nearly three weeks later, which was signed by ninety-seven individual town residents. These residents protested the original petition, because they believed that "the taking up arms for the Removal of any Grievances within this Commonwealth under our present Constitution, ever has been and still is unnecessary." These Brookfield residents reaffirmed their loyalty to the government and stated that they trusted the government to handle the situation appropriately.[40]

Meanwhile, as news of the government's plans began to reach the insurgents, they continued their efforts to recruit and organize a force and determine a response. At a meeting in Pelham on January 15, the regulators put out a call to neighboring towns to send troops and supplies to aid their resistance. They did so because the government not only had refused to respond to their various petitions but was going to "crush the power of the people at one bold stroke, and render them incapable of ever opposing the cruel power, Tyranny, hereafter." According to the regulators, the government was going to try and hunt down those in opposition in order to force them to "an unconditional submission, and their leaders with an infamous punishment." Because of this provocation, the regulators called for the people of Hampshire

County to prepare and send troops with "ten days' provision" to the town of Pelham on January 19.[41]

## Showdown in Springfield

In early January, as Governor Bowdoin and General Lincoln began to mobilize a militia force in and around Boston, many regulators converged on the army barracks in Rutland, Massachusetts. The barracks would afford the regulators a shelter where they could gather in numbers, and its location only twelve miles northwest of Worcester meant that they could reach the Worcester courthouse in a few short hours of marching. In the midst of their preparations, the regulators were visited by Rufus Putnam. Putnam was no supporter of the regulation, but during the Revolutionary War Daniel Shays had served under him as a captain, and Putnam hoped that he could convince Shays to abandon the regulators and seek a government pardon.[42] On January 8, 1787, Putnam wrote to Governor Bowdoin from Rutland to tell him about a recent conversation with Shays. When asked by Putnam why he had become involved in the insurgency, Shays told him that the only reason he had taken command of a group of regulators back in September in Springfield was "to prevent the shedding of blood." If that were true, Putnam asked Shays, then why did he continue to play such a prominent role in the movement after the court closing in Springfield, especially after the Act of Indemnity was passed on November 15? Shays replied that after Springfield the government was trying to arrest and punish him, and "I was determined not to be taken." Shays told Putnam that the regulators had marched in early December because they did not realize that an act of indemnity had been passed. Finally, Shays denied being the leader of the regulators. He said that all of the decisions to arm and organize themselves to close the courts were deliberative and reached by consensus, where he was simply one among many. In fact, Shays said, he had recently refused to lead regulators to Worcester in anticipation of the court session planned for January 23, but "Upon my refusing to act they have chose a Committee, who have ordered the men to march." Putnam urged Shays to abandon the insurgents: Go to Boston to "throw yourself upon the mercy and under the protection of Government." Shays refused, saying that without a pardon, it was too much of a gamble. Putnam then tried to convince Shays that if he were to go to Boston, the government would never go through with a trial and execution, and even if it did, Putnam offered to be executed in Shays's place. Shays responded that the government would never agree to such an offer, and besides, he said, "I don't want you hanged." Putnam reported this conversation to the governor because he believed that Shays might be convinced to abandon the regulators if he could be assured that he would not be punished.[43]

Bowdoin wrote back to Putnam to inform him that he had shared his letter with his council, and its members had agreed that if Shays abandoned the regulators, "he shall be protected by Government." Shays would not receive a blanket pardon, but the governor said that if he were to be convicted of a crime in court, "you may . . . assure him he shall receive a pardon from the Governor and Council." Bowdoin urged Putnam to be discreet, and not "open yourself to Shays unless you have reason to think he is sincere and there is a high probability of Success."[44] Bowdoin's letter is dated January 17, six days before the court in Worcester was scheduled to open, and two days before General Lincoln's army planned to begin its march. Putnam would later write to Bowdoin that there had been no opportunity to make the offer to Shays before the arrival of Lincoln's army in Worcester, and by that point it seemed too late to do any good.[45] On the same day that Bowdoin wrote to Putnam, an article appeared in the *Massachusetts Centinel*, a Boston newspaper, claiming to have heard from someone else who had served in the army with Shays and had recently visited him. This other eyewitness said that he had gone to Shays's house (which he described as "a stye, it having much more the appearance of a den for brutes than a habitation of men") and found Shays in the process of organizing an army that he claimed was ten thousand men strong. According to this article, the regulators planned to close the court at Worcester before marching the army on to Boston, where it would rain fire down into the city and "*destroy the nest of devils, who by their influence, make the Court enact what laws they please.*"[46]

While information and rumors of the regulators' plans swirled in Boston and other eastern Massachusetts communities, the regulators appear to have encouraged sympathetic towns to petition the legislature not to send troops to Worcester. The petitions that began in late December continued through the month of January and into February, as towns supportive of the regulator cause pleaded with the government to consider regulator demands and not respond with force. In the month of January alone, at least eighteen towns sent petitions to the legislature. For example, on January 17, the people of Sutton stated that they believed the regulators had promised not to obstruct the workings of the court any more. While the Sutton petitioners claimed that they "have never taken any active part" in closing the courts, they hoped that the government would not send troops to Worcester. Sutton then warned what would happen if the government sent a force to capture the regulators: the "said Body of men . . . will imbody & defend themselves at the risk of their lives." Sutton hoped that the government to not allow "such a melancholly Consequence."[47]

On the same day, the regulators themselves sent a petition from the barracks at Rutland. They informed the governor that after several meetings they had "Agreed not to obstruct" the court session planned the next week in Worcester, "Provided your Excellency and Honnours Will be Pleased to Withhold your Troops from Marching." In addition, the committee wanted an assurance that those men who had taken part in previous court closures would not face charges. Finally, the petition noted that the regulators were "in full expectation that the next session of the General Court will redress all our Real Grievances and Restore peace and Harmony to this Commonwealth."[48] The Rutland petition was delivered to the Governor's Council by two prominent members of the convention movement, John Fessenden and Samuel Hamilton, who must have raced to deliver it on January 18, one day before General Lincoln's troops were scheduled to begin their march to Worcester.[49] Another politician sympathetic to the regulators was Amos Singletary of Sutton, who also directly appealed to the Governor's Council to stop the militia. At this point, however, Bowdoin and other government officials were committed to a decisive showdown that they hoped would end the insurgency once and for all.

Back in the fall of 1786, the calls for militia forces had been most successful in and around the city of Boston, and when Governor Bowdoin made the proclamation asking for troops in January, those communities again responded most enthusiastically. In the week between Governor Bowdoin's call for troops and General Lincoln's departure for Worcester, about two thousand militia troops from Suffolk, Middlesex, and Essex enlisted and made their way to General Lincoln's camp in Roxbury to prepare for the march to Worcester. Like the rank-and-file members of the regulator forces, most members of the state militia were young men in their teens or early twenties. The difference is that most of the militia forces came from towns that were more commercially oriented, and it is likely that they opposed both the

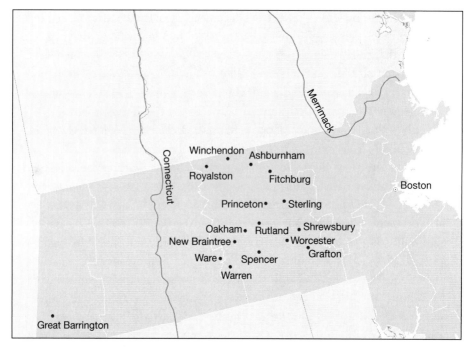

Massachusetts towns sending petitions to Governor Bowdoin between December 21, 1786, and January 25, 1787. Source: Petitions from Shays' Rebellion Collection, American Antiquarian Society.

methods and the platform of the agrarian regulators. In the interior, militia mobilization was not as enthusiastic, but forces were formed in Worcester, Hampshire, and Berkshire counties. For example, on January 18, militia colonel and Worcester County sheriff William Greenleaf summoned the two militia companies of the town of Lancaster and told them they were needed to support the government and end the insurgency. According to the *Worcester Magazine*, after Greenleaf had made his case, there was "some calm debate on the subject," and then he "requested all who were friends of government, to follow him." The paper noted approvingly that nearly everyone, "with very few exceptions," were willing to march to Worcester to ensure that the courts stayed open.[50] In Hampshire County, meanwhile, William Shepard was able to organize a twelve-hundred-man force, largely from Connecticut River market towns like Northampton, Springfield, and Hatfield.

At six-thirty in the morning on Friday, January 19, as a heavy snow began to fall, reveille sounded in the militia camp in Roxbury, and approximately two thousand troops stirred to begin the three-day march to Worcester. The troops were led by an advance guard of artillery, followed by ammunition and food wagons, and soldiers on horseback and on foot. Lincoln wanted them to march slowly and methodically to Worcester, taking care not to "insult or injure" the civilians in the countryside: "To protect them is our indispensible duty."[51] The forty-mile march took three days to complete, and the force arrived in Worcester without incident the day before the court was scheduled to open. It was joined by units of militia from Worcester County. The next day, January 23, the court session opened without any sign of the regulators.

As Lincoln's troops made their way to Worcester, General Shepard was marshaling the Hampshire County militia force in Springfield. Men began arriving on January 18, and by the next day there were approximately one thousand Hampshire militiamen who had arrived to occupy the arsenal and other government buildings in the town. As he had done back in September, Shepard again broke into the armory without formal approval from Secretary of War Henry Knox in order to ensure that the militia forces were fully armed. As he explained to Governor Bowdoin, Shepard believed himself justified because "it would appear highly absurd the Magazine should fall into enemies hands" if he had waited for Knox's formal permission. In addition to taking guns and ammunition, Shepard also took three four-pound cannon and a howitzer from the federal stores. While his men were fully supplied with weapons from the armory, Shepard was concerned about other supplies, and he still had some nagging doubts about the loyalty of his force. Writing on January 19, Shepard told the governor that he had relied on his personal credit with area merchants in order for his soldiers to have the necessary supplies, and so he asked the governor to make sure that more supplies would arrive soon. He also asked that the governor to send $2,000 cash "by the speediest conveyance," because he wanted his soldiers to have a bonus in advance before the regulators arrived: "I . . . wish to pay a small Sum suppose one Dollar to each private which measure would have a Tendency to give more Satisfaction and even Energy to Government than Ten times that from Three Months Hence."[52]

As the regulators become aware of the size of the force headed for Worcester to defend the court, they eventually decided not to go to Worcester, but rather converge on Springfield. From Berkshire County, about three hundred men led by Eli Parsons marched in the snow to Chicopee, just north of Springfield. At the same time, nearly one thousand regulators from Hampshire County gathered in West Springfield under the command of Luke Day,[53] while another thousand or more regulators were gathering east of Springfield. In Springfield, General Shepard became aware that his force faced insurgents on three sides. On January 22, he reported that the insurgents had gained control of major roads and were seizing provisions and preventing additional militia forces from reaching the militia in Springfield. In the town of Greenville, regulators stopped and seized two militia officers, Colonel Robinson and Oliver Phelps Esq., "and even bayonetted their horses."[54] As Shepard told Bowdoin, the insurgents had set up a "strict guard on the other side of the river about one mile from this, and are very hostile they suffer no man to pass or repass their Sentries at some times & at others let them pass." The insurgents not only posted sentries but also captured several local merchants and store owners and seized grain, meat, and other supplies.

By January 24, Shepard was feeling quite isolated—all of the roads out of Springfield were under control of the insurgents, except for the southern road leading in to Connecticut. He estimated that the total insurgent force was close to two thousand, which was at least eight hundred more than the militia force under his command. By now, the forces arrayed against him in West Springfield and Chicopee were joined by Shays's force, which had entered the town of Palmer (to the east of Springfield). Shepard believed that the insurgents would soon be on their way to dislodge him from the armory: "I am threatened with an Attack hourly."[55] Shepard wrote several letters to Lincoln urging the commander to bring his force from Worcester, but he received no replies: "Shays and Day with their forces have stopped every avenue by which supplies and recruits can be brought to this post. The provisions designed for the support of the troops under my command are now converted to the use of the Insurgents." He told Lincoln that he and his men had about four days' worth of supplies, and if he was not defending the armory, he would try to break through the insurgent lines to join Lincoln, but he recognized that he might have to take action on his own: "If you cannot grant me any reinforcements, or relief, I shall try to work out my own salvation before it is too late."[56]

The next day, January 25, Shepard received ultimatums from two groups of regulators. One came from the camp in West Springfield, signed by Captain Luke Day. Day told Shepard, "The body of the people assembled in arms, adhering to the first principle in nature, self-preservation, do in the most peremptory manner demand" that Shepard's forces lay down their arms and return to their homes.[57] The other petition was sent by Daniel Shays from the town of Wilbraham, about eight miles east of Springfield. In it, Shays promised to have the insurgent parties return home if the government pardoned those who had taken part in recent court actions, freed those already in jail, and disbanded the militia. If Governor Bowdoin agreed to such steps, then Shays promised that the regulators would remain peaceful and wait for the spring's elections after which they hoped that the legislature would provide relief "from the Insupportable Burdens thy now Labour under."[58]

In addition to his letter to Shepard, Shays had also sent a message to Day, proposing that they converge on the armory together. Day's response noted that he had sent Shepard an ultimatum and would not attack before receiving a reply, which meant that Day's force would not advance until the next day. However, Shays never received Day's message because it was intercepted by Shepard's men.[59] Later that afternoon, while Luke Day's force remained in West Springfield, the regulators under the command of Shays linked up with Eli Parsons's force in Chicopee to advance on the militia in Springfield. The deep snow required that the fifteen hundred or so regulators had to march in narrow bands as they approached the hill leading up to the armory, which was protected by a militia force of between a thousand and twelve hundred men, along with the cannon and howitzer that had been removed from the armory. When the regulators got to within a half mile of the armory, they were met by two of Shepard's aides—William Lyman and Samuel Buffington—who were sent to find out what Shays wanted. Shays told the men that "he wanted barracks, & barracks he would have & stores." The aides replied that if he wanted them, he would have to "purchase them dear."[60] They warned the regulators that if they refused to stop, the militia would fire on them. At least one prominent regulator, Adam Wheeler, responded by saying "That is all we want by God."[61]

When the regulators continued the march, Shepard ordered that two cannon be fired over the heads of the advancing men, hoping the warning shots would persuade them to halt their advance. The shots were fired, but the regulators continued to march, as the artillery men reloaded their weapons. When the regulators got to within one hundred yards of the armory, Shepard ordered the artillery to fire directly at the oncoming regulators. Multiple shots were fired from the cannon and howitzer, which sprayed grapeshot into the ranks of the regulators, who scattered without firing a weapon.[62] One eyewitness noted that the regulator leaders, including Daniel Shays, "tried to hold them together," but could not rally the regulator force. Other than the shots fired by the government artillery, no guns were discharged. The artillery fire killed three insurgents, mortally wounded another, and injured several more. The government militia suffered only one injury, when one of the men operating the cannon was accidently hit and suffered the loss of both arms and his eyesight.[63] As the regulators fled, and with nightfall approaching General Shepard decided that the militia would not give chase, even though he told Bowdoin that he could have followed with his infantry and two field pieces and "would have killed the greater part of his whole army within twenty five minutes."[64]

## Petersham

The next day, anticipating another attack and seemingly without reinforcements, Shepard had the militia construct defensive works surrounding the armory.[65] But the regulators did not attack. In West Springfield, the regulator force under Luke Day remained in place, while those regulators who had marched on the armory had retreated north along the Connecticut River toward the town of Ludlow. An eyewitness noted that some of the insurgents deserted, while most marched into Chicopee on January 27.[66] Two days earlier in Worcester, General Lincoln had received word of an imminent attack on Shepard's militia in Springfield, and he decided to march most of his force there. Lincoln's army began to arrive in the city on the afternoon of January 27, and after taking time to find out where the insurgents were, and to give his forces a brief rest, Lincoln gave orders to go after the insurgents. Four regiments of Lincoln's militia, along with troops on horseback and four artillery pieces, marched across the frozen Connecticut River in an attempt to capture the regulators in West Springfield. The insurgents had posted a guard at the ferry house on the West Springfield side of the river, and when the regulators there saw the militia on the march, they "turned out and left the pass open" as they retreated. At the West Springfield meetinghouse, they stopped briefly for a "show of force," but then "retired in utmost confusion and disorder."[67] Militia troops on horseback attempted to capture the fleeing insurgents, but by "crossing the fields and taking to the woods," most insurgents in West Springfield were able to escape. Meanwhile, another part of the militia marched up the ice on the Connecticut River to Chicopee. The regulators there marched north to South Hadley, on their way to Amherst.

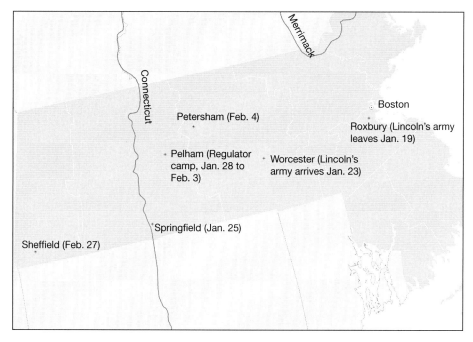

The conflict in the winter of 1787.

The bulk of the regulator force then made its way into the hill town of Pelham. This was a center of regulator activity, as well as the home of Daniel Shays. The regulators could expect support from the townspeople, and Pelham's two hills provided them with a chance to establish a defensive position against the government militia. According to the *Worcester Magazine*, the regulators "posted strong guards on the heights of land; the approach of a regular army to these heights is very difficult, particularly at this season of the year."[68] While the regulators settled into Pelham, Lincoln's army established camp in the town of Hadley, ten miles west of the regulators. Before Lincoln made it to Hadley, he was approached by a "Committee called Mediators, from several towns," who wanted to try and prevent further armed conflict by asking Lincoln to retreat, but he refused. Lincoln recognized the strong defensive position of the insurgents in Pelham, so he did not immediately risk a direct attack. Rather, he sent a message under a flag of truce with three representatives, including Rufus Putnam. The message indicated that the regulator position was hopeless and that Lincoln was ready to recommend clemency for any of the rank-and-file regulators who agreed to surrender. Lincoln directed the letter to "Captain Shays and the Officers commanding the men in arms against the Government of this Commonwealth." In the proposal, Lincoln requested Shays and the other regulator leaders to tell their privates that "if they will instantly lay down their arms, surrender themselves to government, and take and subscribe the oath of allegiance to this Commonwealth, they shall be recommended to the General Court for mercy."[69] According to an eyewitness account, "Shays treated them with civility, and, after a long consultation with his officers, returned an answer to General Lincoln's letter."[70] The regulators rejected Lincoln's proposal and made a counteroffer. They wanted a pardon for all insurgents and a truce until the legislature had a chance to respond to the latest regulator petition.[71] Lincoln refused this proposal and instead had copies of his own proposal "printed and dispersed in the country."[72] At least one newspaper account suggested that Lincoln's actions led "great numbers" to abandon the insurgents and take the oath of allegiance. Despite Lincoln's efforts, a sizable regulator force, numbering in the hundreds, remained in Pelham.

As Lincoln's army and the regulators faced one another, some minor skirmishes erupted nearby. In New Braintree, about fifteen miles east of Pelham, a group of insurgents captured two men who had come to the town of Leicester on February to collect a debt. The two men, John Stanton and Samuel Flagg, were brought to New Braintree and imprisoned in a local tavern. A force of 120 government soldiers came to free the men, but the soldiers were shot at by some insurgents who had "placed themselves behind some fences." The insurgents fired upon the government men, hitting one man in the arm and hand and the other in the knee. The government forces chased the men to Rutland, where they were able to capture some of them.[73]

After two days of relative stalemate, in which more efforts at a truce were unsuccessfully attempted, General Lincoln decided that he needed to take some decisive action. It was true that the regulators had a strong defensive position in Pelham, but Lincoln began to worry about what might happen when the thirty-day enlistment of the militia forces expired. He did not want to risk a loss of forces if a significant number of men decided that they wanted to return home. So, on February 2, Lincoln sent out scouts to reconnoiter the insurgents' position in Pelham, and he began to make plans for an attack. By the following afternoon—perhaps sensing the impending attack—the insurgents began to leave Pelham for the town of Petersham, which was about thirty miles to the north and east. A heavy snowfall had taken place on February 2, but the next day was clear, if cold. That evening, Lincoln became aware of the regulator retreat and directed his force to follow. Lincoln planned to have his men march for several miles into the night and then rest for a few hours before attempting to catch up with the insurgents the next day. During the night, however, the calm conditions gave way to a violent blizzard and freezing temperatures. As it happened, there were no towns between Pelham and Petersham where Lincoln's men could stop for rest and shelter, and rather than stop on the road where they would remain exposed to the brutal storm, Lincoln decided to press on all night in an effort to reach Petersham.

The regulators, who had a several hours' head start, reached Petersham in the early morning hours of February 4, where they sought shelter among the townspeople. Exhausted and thinking that the militia would have to wait out the storm, most were still asleep when Lincoln's army made its surprise appearance after sunrise. The militia had marched thirty miles overnight pulling artillery pieces through a blinding snowstorm. According to militia soldier Thomas Thompson, the blizzard turned the march into an ordeal which made travel extremely difficult for the men: "The wind rose to a great height and blew snow with excessive violence . . . The old paths were all filled up immediately. The wind and snow seemed to come in whirls and eddies and penetrated the all of my clothes and filled my eyes, ears, neck, and everything else which, added to the severe cold, made the march distressing as words can describe it." When they arrived, a great many suffered from frostbite. The heavy snow had forced the militia to march in narrow rows, and if the regulators had been expecting them, they would have been able to fire down upon them when they approached. However, many of the regulators were also suffering the effects of exposure and exhaustion.[74] One government trooper observed that "the movement was so unexpected and sudden, that they were immediately thrown into disorder . . . [They] had not time to call in their out parties or even their guards."[75] At Petersham, the main insurgent force was routed, and upward of 150 regulators were captured. However, many individuals had escaped, and smaller bands of regulators remained in Berkshire County.

# 5 Governing the Regulators and Regulating Government

THE DAY BEFORE Lincoln's army caught up to the regulators in Petersham, the Massachusetts state legislature began meeting in Boston in an effort to respond to this new stage in the conflict. In the aftermath of Petersham, government officials and militia commanders were faced with various challenges. First, the militia troops authorized by Governor Bowdoin would have to be paid for, and the Boston merchants who had advanced a loan would have to be reimbursed. The state treasury was essentially empty, and officials would have to balance the continued need for troops with their cost. Second, an unknown number of regulators—including most of the men whom authorities considered regulator leaders—had fled Petersham and had made their way out of the state. The governor and legislature would need to seek assistance from neighboring states and Vermont in an effort to track down and capture these escaped men. Third, small bands of insurgents remained active, especially in Berkshire County, and they would attempt to seek cover across the state line in New York. Most of Lincoln's force would be shifted there to meet up with militia forces already in the area. Fourth, the most complex question had to do with the fate of the defeated regulators: How should they be punished, and what should be done to reincorporate them into the body politic? Some government officials, most notably Samuel Adams, argued that citizenship in a republic required a level of commitment and self-sacrifice considerably greater than being a subject under a king or queen, and those citizens who threatened the order and stability of their own republics should pay the ultimate price: "In monarchies," Adams said, "the crime of treason and rebellion may admit of being pardoned or lightly punished; but the man who dares to rebel against the laws of a republic ought to suffer death."[1]

## Ending the Insurgency

The first action of the legislature—made on the same day that the militia arrived in Petersham—was an official declaration that Massachusetts was in a state of open rebellion. According to the legislature, in the fall it had tried to do everything it could to address the concerns of the people. Now that the insurgents had organized to take up arms, it was clear to the legislature that the insurgent leaders had a "settled determination to subvert the Constitution and put an end to the Government of this Commonwealth."[2] The fact that the insurgents organized themselves into armed groups was "subversive of all order and government." As a result, the legislature believed that it was its responsibility to declare "that a horrid and unatural REBELLION and WAR, has been openly and traiterously raised and levied against this Commonwealth." Given the gravity of the situation, the legislature pledged that it would "exert and bring forth, all the power of the Commonwealth" to put the rebellion down. This declaration reinforced the governor's authority as commander in chief to raise additional militia forces or declare martial law if he deemed it necessary.[3]

In addition to recognizing and supporting the actions of Governor Bowdoin in responding to the crisis, and those who volunteered for the militia to put down the uprising, the legislature also praised "the patriotic zeal of a number of private Citizens, who have chearfully advanced their money in aid to Government." The legislature pledged that it would make sure that the loan was paid back as soon as possible and directed £40,000 of the state's impost and excise tax to pay for the troops and supplies.[4] Two days later it specified the pay for soldiers in the militia, noting that the pay was to be "discharged by the Treasurer in Specie, with all the speed that is practicable."[5] The original term of the militia force was one month, and in mid-February the legislature made a commitment to fund fifteen hundred troops for four months. It quickly realized, however, that there was not enough funds from the impost and excise tax to pay for troops and supplies, and so the government was forced to solicit another direct loan from wealthy Bostonians. Bowdoin himself personally loaned another £500.[6]

Back in Hampshire County, General Lincoln was well aware of the financial limitations of the legislature, and he hoped to reduce the size of his force as soon as possible. In addition to the financial cost, Lincoln was concerned about the impact that a couple of thousand soldiers might have on the morale and loyalty of the people in nearby towns. The aggressive tactics and haughty attitude of the cavalry units that had made forays into Groton and Shrewsbury in the fall had angered the countryside and led many to conclude that the regulator claims of a tyrannical government were real. From the time the militia force left the camp at Roxbury on January 19, Lincoln showed concern that the men under his command not bother the people in the towns through which they traveled. Part of this concern may have also been colored by Lincoln's views of the common soldiers under his command. As Lincoln wrote to the governor, the men in the field "are a class of citizens who cannot be retained long in the field without public as well as private injury."[7] Most of the rank-and-file militia volunteers were young men from communities around Boston, and they had faced long marches in extremely uncomfortable winter weather among civilian populations that were not necessarily happy to see them in their communities. On February 7, in the town of Amherst, Lincoln disapproved when his officers allowed their soldiers "to leave their Ranks and to fill the houses near the Road."[8] The soldiers must have welcomed this chance to briefly escape the harsh winter conditions and warm themselves. But Lincoln recognized that government troops would have to tread lightly or weaken the very loyalty they hoped to rebuild. In the days following Petersham, several of the militia soldiers were charged with plundering and faced a hastily convened court-martial. The men were found guilty, but General Lincoln was upset that the punishment they received from the court officers was what he considered mild. Each of the men was sentenced "to have a paper on their Breasts, containing the words, *for plundering*, which they are to wear, passing before the army when paraded having their hats off."[9]

While in the days after Petersham some of Lincoln's time was spent worrying about the impact his troops were having on the local civilian population, his primary concern was to track down and capture the insurgent leaders who had fled on February 4. Within about thirty minutes after their arrival in Petersham that day, the state militia accepted the surrender of about 150 men, while others scattered into the countryside. Many of the rank-and-file regulators probably went back to their homes, hoping to either escape notice or take an oath of allegiance and receive a pardon. However, most prominent regulator leaders realized that if they were captured, they would stand trial for treason and face execution if convicted. Therefore, many who fled Petersham traveled north through the towns of Athol and Warwick, and then made their way to the New Hampshire state line, about twenty miles from Petersham. On February 8, several hundred insurgents, including Daniel Shays, were seen outside the town of Chesterfield in southwest New Hampshire. About one hundred of the men were in a group, and they were followed by a scattering of two hundred more. According to the eyewitness, the men "appeared in a miserable abject state."[10] Many of the men headed to nearby Vermont, where they sought out friends or family to take them in and prevent them from being captured. For example, regulator leaders Luke and Elijah Day traveled to Marlborough, Vermont, to stay with a brother who lived there.[11]

Many of the insurgents who traveled to Vermont soon sent word to have family members travel with them. Government observers and informants noticed hundreds of people leading "livestock, household furniture, and all the moveable property" they owned across the Massachusetts line.[12] One of the reasons many stayed is that they received support for sympathetic local farmers, even as Massachusetts officials sent parties into Vermont in order to capture high-profile regulators. For example, William Shepard's aide Samuel Buffington led twenty men on horseback into Brattleboro, Vermont, after receiving intelligence that Luke Day and others were hiding out there. Buffington received support from the local sheriff, but many in the town were opposed to Buffington and his men. They let Day and other insurgents know that he was being pursued, and then they formed an armed force of about seventy, which threatened and insulted Buffington and his men and caused them to retreat.[13]

As they were returning to Massachusetts, Buffington's men encountered a party of insurgents led by Jason Parmenter of Hubbardstown, who were heading to Vermont carrying provisions on a sleigh. According to Buffington, when Parmenter realized that he had run into a militia force, he ordered his men to fire, and two men aimed at militiaman Aaron Whitney. Fortunately for Whitney, the guns misfired. Meanwhile, another militiaman, Jacob Walker, jumped onto the back of Parmenter's sleigh. Parmenter shot Walker, who died a short time later, while Parmenter and his men fled. Because the snow was deep and the woods were thick, some of members of the militia force dismounted, put on snowshoes, and followed on foot, while others followed later on horseback. They crossed back over into Vermont and were able to capture Parmenter and bring him back to Massachusetts for trial.[14]

While Parmenter was captured, no other prominent regulators were taken out of Vermont, despite the efforts of Buffington and Royall Tyler, who was serving as an aide to General Lincoln. When the call for militia volunteers was made in January 1787, the then twenty-nine-year-old Tyler jumped at the chance to make a little money and have an adventure. Born into a wealthy family, Tyler had graduated from Harvard in 1776, but he squandered a fortune and gained a reputation as a heavy drinker and womanizer during college and for some years after. After college, he trained as a lawyer, eventually settling in Braintree where he acquired a large farm and sought John Adams's daughter Abigail's hand in marriage. But his farm was a failure, and eventually Abigail spurned his advances. Despite little military experience, he was named as Lincoln's aide de camp, and following Petersham he traveled between Vermont and New York wearing disguises and concocting schemes to trap and capture escaped regulators. (Later that spring, while in New York City, Tyler drew on these experiences as inspiration in writing the first American play, titled *The Contrast*.)[15] Tyler sent Lincoln dispatches in which he provided information about the whereabouts of regulator leaders and suggested that he had a network of informants and spies who were helping him gather information that would lead to the capture of the escaped men. For example, in mid-February he received reports that Daniel Shays's wife had arrived in Bennington, Vermont, near the New York border. He told General Lincoln that he was having her watched with the hope that she would bring them to Shays himself.[16] His informants were able to seize Adam Wheeler near Bennington, but resistance from neighboring farmers allowed Wheeler to escape: "At White Creek Adam Wheeler was taken by one of my emissaries the day before yesterday, carried two miles & an half, & then rescued by forty odd Yorkers who carried him back in triumph to a large mob."[17]

Militia commanders Lincoln and Shepard became increasingly frustrated by the unwillingness of Vermont authorities to aid in the capture of escaped regulators. Following the events in Petersham, Governor Bowdoin had contacted the governors of neighboring states to ask for their assistance in tracking down and turning over men who may have escaped into their states, and he issued rewards for the capture of some prominent regulators. The governors of New Hampshire and Connecticut both responded with clear indications that they would provide as much help as they could. But in Vermont and New York, the response was far less robust. On February 27, Lincoln told Bowdoin that he had written the governor of New York to tell him that as "long as the Rebels shall find an Asylum in the neighboring states," it would impossible to "fully quell the Spirit of Rebellion."[18]

By March 2, General Shepard was angry that New York and Vermont seemed to be doing nothing to help them, and in fact people in those states appeared "to comfort, [and] supply with provisions . . . arms and ammunition, those who set our laws and constitution at defiance." If that were allowed to continue, Shepard warned, then "the business of crushing the present rebellion, and reducing the rebels to their duty and allegiance, is but begun." He believed that the state would need to mobilize a much larger number of troops for a considerable length of time, not just to quash the rebellion but also to ensure that loyal citizens would be "safe from murder and depredation." As long as insurgents could slip across state lines and be free from capture, they would be able to wage "a savage, predatory war upon the citizens of the Commonwealth."[19]

What were the plans of the escaped insurgents? Informants reported that a group of insurgents had traveled to Quebec to seek arms and support from the British governor there. At first, the men were given a promise of support, but no weapons materialized.[20] Another report indicated that regulator leaders had sought out Revolutionary War hero Ethan Allen in Vermont, and asked if he would become their leader. Allen had been critical of the action of the Massachusetts government, yet he was unwilling to tie his fate to that of the escaped regulators.[21] For some regulator leaders in Vermont, there was a desire to regroup and repay the Massachusetts military for the defeat they had suffered. In mid-February, regulator leader Eli Parsons wrote an open letter that called for a new mobilization. Parsons made an appeal to the disaffected not to give up, even though their forces had fled: "Friends and fellow sufferers. Will you now tamely suffer your arms to be taken from you—your estates to be confiscated, and even swear to support a Constitution and form of Government, and likewise a code of laws, which common sense and your consciences declare to be iniquitous and cruel?" Referring to the artillery fire at Springfield on January 25, Parsons wondered how people could allow yeoman farmers to be "cut to pieces by the cruel and merciless tools of tyrannical power, and not resent it even unto unrelenting bloodshed?" According to Parsons, the people should rise up and defeat General Lincoln the way that they had defeated British General Burgoyne at the pivotal battle of Saratoga back in 1777.[22] While some men like Parsons did hope for a new regulator force to rise, others likely hoped just to avoid capture and trial. At the same time that Parsons was writing his incendiary plea, a government informant reported that Daniel Shays was "wary in his conduct, passing under different names, lodging in various houses, and keeping a centinel at some distance of his place of abode, and was determined not to be taken alive."[23]

At the same time that he coordinated efforts to capture regulators in Vermont, Lincoln brought the bulk of his militia force out of Hampshire and into far-western Berkshire County, where groups of insurgents had been harassing supporters of government. While most groups of active regulators had converged on Springfield by January 21, there were some regulators in Berkshire County who had not been able to join the others, and they had several encounters with groups of government supporters and the Berkshire militia led by General John Patterson of Lenox. On the same day that regulators marched on the armory in Springfield, a group of insurgents encountered government supporters near Sheffield and was able to take two prisoners. The insurgents tried to capture prominent lawyer and government supporter Theodore Sedgwick, but he was able to escape. The next day two groups of government supporters met near Sheffield, commandeered the only artillery piece in the county, and proceeded to the town of Stockbridge, where they met a group of about one hundred insurgents, many of whom were unarmed. The government supporters fired a cannon shot in warning, and the insurgents retreated, only to assemble in a larger force the next day in West Stockbridge. Militia commander John Patterson was able to assemble a force of several hundred, which approached West Stockbridge from three different roads, and surrounded and captured eighty-four insurgents.[24] Fifteen of the men considered insurgent leaders were kept in jail, while the others were allowed to return to their homes after taking an oath of allegiance. A short time later, another showdown between insurgent forces and the militia led to a negotiation where General Patterson convinced the insurgents to give up by promising that he would intercede on their behalf in an effort to ensure that any future trials would take place in Berkshire County.[25] On February 5, Patterson wrote to Lincoln that the regulators were still quite active in Berkshire County and that they were receiving encouragement from someone who had crossed the state line into New York, who was "endeavoring by the propagation of every falsehood he could invent, to rouse the inhabitants to reinforce his party here." Patterson hoped that Lincoln would be able to "immediately dispatch a body of men" to come to Berkshire County.[26]

Lincoln's force traveled west to Berkshire, but most of the troops were dismissed on February 21 when their enlistments were up, although some remained, and reinforcements would arrive. The militia's task was complicated by the ability of insurgents to cross the state line into New York where they were sheltered by family or friends, and where they could plan additional actions in Berkshire. The most dramatic foray began in the evening of February 26, when a group of more than one hundred insurgents gathered in New Lebanon, New York, before marching overnight across the state line, passing through the towns of New Canaan and West Stockbridge, and arriving in Stockbridge at about four o'clock in the morning on February 27. The men divided into small parties and began banging on the doors of homes, offices, and stores of those known to support the government, including the law office of Theodore Sedgwick and the general store owned by Silas Pepoon. If refused admittance, they broke down the doors or windows to gain entrance and threatened the people inside. Once inside, they gathered guns and ammunition, cash, and provisions and began taking prisoners. All told, the insurgents took fifty-one prisoners in Stockbridge, but let some of them go before marching toward Great Barrington.[27] After arriving there they took nineteen more hostages, broke open the jails and released the debtors, and then began to march with their prisoners toward the town of Sheffield. As night began to fall, they were overtaken by a militia force led by Colonel John Ashley. When the insurgents recognized that the militia had caught up to them, they fired once at them and then put their prisoners between them and the militia: "The general cry was, push on the prisoners." According to one witness, each side fired twice as the militia approached, and according to Colonel Ashley, "The troops under my command advanced rapidly towards them & a warm fire commenced for about six minutes." Only one of the prisoners was killed, probably by militia gunfire, although one

insolent menaces have been and still are in circulation in those places at least where none of the troops of government have appeared, and inflammatory letters have been handed about to prevent the evil spirits of sedition and rebellion from evaporating." Shepard believed that a significant militia presence would be required for a while at least. These forces would be necessary "to rivet in their minds a compleat conviction of the force of government and the necessity of an entire submission to the laws."[32]

While militia commanders emphasized the need right after Petersham to maintain a show of government force, many towns countered with petitions that pleaded with the legislature to show clemency toward the insurgents, and town petitions highlighted a fear that government action might lead to more violence. In early February, the town of Hopkinton wrote to the governor and legislature to ask for a pardon for the insurgents because, even though it disagreed with those who took up arms against the government, the town believed that most insurgents did so because they were operating "under the mistaken notion of its being the only way to obtain redress of certain grievances." While seeking a pardon for the insurgents, it also tried to explain why they had been unwilling to join the government militia under General Lincoln. They did not serve because many of the insurgents were from families that had once lived in the town but had moved further west to settle in new towns. As a result, "many of us have Brothers & near Relations, among the Insurgents." They wanted to reaffirm their support and allegiance to the government, but they also wanted to make clear that they could not willingly take part "in pronouncing the Sentence of Death on our Breatheren who have arisen in arms against Government," because "nature recoils at the thought of being Personally the Executioners of that Sentence."[33] The town of Paxton's petition for a unconditional pardon emphasized its belief that the problems in the countryside were real and that the insurgents were responding to such problems not in a devious way, but only because they felt it was the way to obtain relief: "as we think that allowance ought to be made on account of the Ignorance & great distresses of the People in General."[34]

In addition to looking backward toward the causes that might have led would-be insurgents to take desperate action, some towns also anticipated the crafting of policies that would lead to the most durable and peaceful reunion. As the town of Lunenburg put it in its petition of February 19: "A military Force may kill, capture or disperse the Body in Arms against Government; but will it restore their alienated affections? Chains may restrain

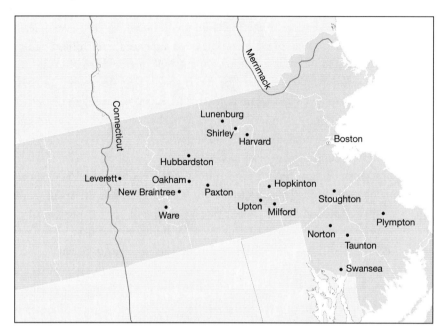

Massachusetts towns sending petitions to Governor Bowdoin between January 27 and February 19, 1787. Source: Petitions from Shays' Rebellion Collection, American Antiquarian Society.

a Madman from Acts of Violence and Outrage; but they will not remove the Cause of his Insanity."[35] The residents of Lunenburg believed that the underlying factors that had led to the rebellion had not been adequately dealt with, and while punishing those deemed responsible might restore a semblance of order, it would allow the underlying conditions to continue to fester. The town of Shirley also thought that a pardon would not just restore order but that it would help the former insurgents get reincorporated into the political community: a pardon would help make "much better subjects than they would be if subdued by force."[36]

In February and March, the state legislature took steps to respond to the rebellion, and overall it emphasized punishment rather than relief. On February 16, it clarified the pardon process by passing the Disqualification Act. Anyone who had taken up arms against the government, or had given any insurgent "aid, comfort, or support . . . with intent to encourage the opposition to government," needed to receive a pardon for his actions. Pardons were not available for those insurgents who had taken on any kind of leadership role: members of the legislature or holder of any state office, officers in the insurgent armies, or prominent advisers to the insurgents. Also denied pardons was anyone who had taken an earlier oath but then rejoined the insurgents, or anyone who had fired a weapon at government troops or supporters. Insurgents who did not fit any of these categories were eligible for a pardon in which they would come before a justice of the peace, pay a registration fee, turn in their guns, and take the oath of allegiance. Those granted a pardon were punished by being disqualified from voting, serving as a town or state official, or working as a teacher or a seller of "Spirituous liquors" for up to three years (although they could receive these rights as early as May 1788 if they could show their "unequivocal attachment to the Government").[37] Ten days later, town selectmen were empowered to remove the names of anyone they suspected of supporting the rebellion from jury lists for one year.[38]

A few weeks later, the legislature expanded the possibility of pardon by naming a three-person commission of Benjamin Lincoln, Senate president Samuel Phillips, and Boston merchant and state representative Samuel A. Otis. This commission would go to Middlesex, Worcester, Hampshire, and Berkshire counties in order to interview those who had not been eligible for earlier pardons, and if the commissioners were convinced that the men were "duly penitent for their crimes, and properly disposed to return their allegiance to the Commonwealth," they could offer them a pardon. This commission also had the authority to restore the civil rights of pardoned individuals that had been taken away by the disqualification act. The only men whom the commissioners were not authorized to pardon were Daniel Shays, Adam Wheeler, Eli Parsons, and Luke Day, along with others who had been part of the insurgent "Council of War" since January 20, anyone who had led troops that fired on government forces, or who did the actual firing, and finally anyone else who had a warrant out for his arrest.[39]

As the commissioners made their way across the western counties, the state legislature did enact a handful of mild reforms that had been called for by many town and county petitions in the previous summer and fall. In response to the criticism of high court costs, the legislature reduced the cost of many fees associated with court actions, and it also responded to calls for reducing the pay of government officials by passing legislation that reduced Governor Bowdoin's annual salary from £1,100 to £800. However, Bowdoin vetoed the bill, arguing that the legislature did not have the constitutional authority to make such a reduction.[40] By the end of April, the three commissioners submitted their report to the legislature. All together, they offered indemnity to 790 men. They had gone from town to town and, upon arrival in a town, interviewed anyone who believed he was entitled to a pardon. The person had to bring affidavits from two men of unquestioned loyalty claiming that he "is duly penitent for his crime, properly disposed to return to the allegiance of the State, and to discharge the duty of a faithful Citizen thereof."[41] Most of these were pardoned unconditionally. A few were placed on temporary restrictions, and a few others were denied relief and turned over to be tried by the Supreme Judicial Court.

## Judging the Governors and the Governed

Part of the impetus for this commission came from Benjamin Lincoln himself. While Lincoln did want swift and serious punishment meted out to the leaders of the regulation, he was concerned that too many people were being held in county jails, making them targets for rescue attempts.[42] In addition, Lincoln worried that imposing penalties on pardoned insurgents made them less willing to become fully loyal supporters of government, and he thought such penalties were contrary to the spirit of representative government. As Lincoln wrote to Henry Knox in March, it was entirely appropriate for the state to use everything at its disposal to "crush the Rebellion." But once the rebels had been defeated, the state should do what it could to welcome its disaffected citizens back into the fold. Lincoln argued that it was the responsibility of the legislature to "to reclaim its citizens, to bring them back fully to a sense of their Duty, and to establish anew those principles which led them to embrace the Government with affection."[43] Taking away one's right to vote or serve in office sent the wrong message, according to Lincoln. He supposed that the legislature had originally insisted on that punishment because it feared that insurgents might gain power through elections that they were denied by the state militia, but he did not see the logic of that fear. As Lincoln put it to Knox: "The influence of those people is so fully checked that we have nothing to apprehend from them now, but their individual Votes . . . Admit that some of these very people should obtain a seat in the Assembly the next year, we have nothing to fear from the Measure: so far from that, I think it would produce the most salutary Effects." The rapid reinclusion of former insurgents into full citizenship was the best way to rebuild their allegiance to the state. In fact, Lincoln argued, the civil rights of former insurgents should be restored as quickly as possible because "I believe it to be the only way which can be adopted to make them good Members of Society, and to reconcile them to that government under which we wish them to live."[44]

While Lincoln disliked the Disqualification Act because it threatened to make it more difficult to restore the loyalty of former insurgents, others in Massachusetts were upset because the act seemed like a brazen attempt to disqualify political opponents. Springfield minister Belazeel Howard—who had been a critical if sympathetic observer of the regulators—was outraged by the Disqualifying Act: "By that severe and Tyranical act they Indended at one blow to Intirely cut of[f] all opposition to Bowdoin."[45] Howard was also outraged at the government efforts to round up and prosecute suspected insurgent leaders. As the state legislature crafted its policies regarding pardon and disqualification, state attorney general Robert Treat Paine was dispatched to begin to identify suspects and build cases against those that the government would attempt to put on trial for sedition. Much of the evidence collected by Paine was submitted by local elites against men in their communities. Some of the men indicted by Paine complained that they were being framed by people who did not like them and who were trying to get them in trouble. For Howard, such efforts to prosecute were a mockery of justice because, given the fear of rebellion, "very little Testimony is Necessary towards the Conviction of any one that had in smallest degree assisted or suppos[e]d to have assisted or only countenanced." In addition, because, as Howard put it, "Every man more or less has them who are unfriendly about him," it was easy for Paine to find willing witnesses for the prosecution. Even strong supporters of the government, like lawyer Henry Van Schaack, worried that the cases Paine constructed were built upon personal grudges that colored the testimony of state witnesses: "I fear under the Cloack of patriotism some people give way to the gratification of private resentment."[46]

One of the men targeted for such "resentment" was Berkshire County judge William Whiting. He had been one of the three judges forced by the crowd in Berkshire County on September 12, 1786, to adjourn the court. Whiting had been sympathetic to the protests, and in the days leading up to that court session he had written an essay under the pseudonym Graccus. In it, he argued that the people had reason to be upset with their government, and that "whenever it happens in any Republican Government or Commonwealth that some part of the Citizens have it in their Power by Compulsion to enrich themselves by the same means that impoverishes and depresses some other Orders of People," that government was defective. Among the problems that Whiting saw were the large fees that judges and lawyers received for their work, and Whiting later singled out wealthy lawyer Theodore Sedgwick—who had once been a political ally but had become a rival—as a prime example of someone who profited at the expense of others. In the essay, Whiting went on to say that if people were not able to seek relief from such "incroachments" on their "liberties or properties," then "it is Virtue in them to disturb the government."[47] In the fall, Theodore Sedgwick wrote the governor to tell him that he thought Whiting was undermining government authority, and he believed that Whiting actually played a role in the court closure itself. In February, Whiting was arrested and charged with sedition, and Whiting himself was certain that he was the victim of a vendetta.

During March, April, and May, the Supreme Judicial Court heard cases in Berkshire, Hampshire, Worcester, and Middlesex counties. Court sessions began in the town of Great Barrington in Berkshire County on March 20, and the court sat there until April 6. Most of the cases in Berkshire focused on the actions of men who had taken part in the armed conflict in Sheffield. While sixty men were originally indicted for treason, only six were tried and five convicted. All five of the men convicted were sentenced to death. One of the five, Aaron Knap, a former town clerk of West Stockbridge, was convicted on the evidence that he had been part of Perez Hamlin's "advance guard." Hamlin himself was not brought to trial because he was still recovering from wounds received in the conflict and had the support of doctors who said that he was not physically able to stand trial. Two other men, Nathaniel Austin, from Sheffield, and Peter Wilcox Jr., of the town of Lee, had been identified as men who fired at government forces. Convicted for other reasons were Joseph Williams of New Marlboro, who "was taken in flight with his gun loaded," and Enoch Tyler of Egremont, who was singled out because several days before the episode he had taken the Oath of Allegiance. The final insurgent condemned to death in Berkshire was Samuel Rust of Pittsfield. Rust had not taken part in the Sheffield firefight, but he had been prominent in the fall and winter: he helped to close the court in Springfield in September, "was busy circulating Shays's letter, and in inciting people to go to Worcester to join him, marched himself for that purpose in December, and again in January, carrying thirty men along with him."[48] Judge William Whiting was also found guilty of seditious libel and sentenced to seven months in jail and a £100 fine.[49]

After the court session in Berkshire County closed, sessions were held in Northampton in Hampshire County from April 9 to 21, before moving to Worcester and then Concord in Middlesex County. In Hampshire County, Jason Parmenter and regulator Henry McCullough of Pelham were among the six men who received a death sentence, while Henry Gale in Worcester and Job Shattuck in Middlesex received the only death sentences handed out in those two counties. When the court adjourned on May 5, a total of fourteen men had been sentenced to death, and fifteen had received lesser sentences.

As Attorney General Paine collected evidence and organized cases against suspected insurgents, towns throughout the commonwealth prepared for the annual elections of the governor and legislature. As in previous years, towns would hold votes for governor, lieutenant governor, and the state senate in early April, and they would elect their state representative or representatives in early May. While some individual town results would be occasionally reported in newspapers, the official count would not take place until the legislature gathered in late May. In the contest for governor, John Hancock decided to return to politics, and he ran against Bowdoin in an effort to regain the office from which he had resigned two years earlier. Political observers recognized that this election would be something of a referendum on Bowdoin's actions to quell the uprising. Many of Bowdoin's supporters voiced private concerns that the governor's popularity suffered as people came to see the government response to the insurgency as too vigorous and vindictive.[50]

After the battle in Sheffield on February 25, there were no more armed confrontations between government soldiers and groups of insurgents, but violence would continue to take place into June, especially in Berkshire and Hampshire counties. Many of the attacks that occurred were acts of retribution carried out by a few insurgents against the property or person of prominent supporters of government. Often, the attacks involved arson, as when the potash works of Josiah Woodbridge of Hadley was burned down on March 2. Another merchant, a Pittsfield man, had his barn burned down, while two residents of Sheffield had a store they owned in Nobletown, New York, torched. In early April, fires were set at a general store in Westfield and a glass works in Greenfield.[51] Military leaders were also targeted. In early April, a group of insurgents crossed over from New York in an effort to seize General Benjamin Lincoln, who had come near the border town of

New Lebanon to visit the hot spring there. The general was made aware of the impending abduction, and he escaped before the men arrived.[52] As the officer who authorized the cannon fire against insurgents in Springfield, William Shepard became the target of attacks by people who considered him a murderer responsible for the loss of regulator life. In early April, Shepard received a letter threatening to kill him for his actions on January 25: "William Shepard I write you this to let you know we have determined to kill you. I write in haste for my anger being up to the very heavens and crying aloud for vengance."[53] Two weeks after he received this threat, a small band of insurgents burned fences and woodlands on his property in Westfield. The men then mutilated two of Shepard's horses "by cutting off their ears and digging out their eyes before they were killed."[54]

Sporadic raids and attacks continued into May and June, and raiding parties often began across the state line in New York or Vermont. At the end of a May, a militia commander in Northfield reported that men from Vermont and New Hampshire came into Northfield and "with intention I suppose to attack this town, plunder, and carry of[f] the friends of Government," but they were repulsed. That same evening, some insurgents went to the town of Warwick, where they abducted "Doctor Pomeroy and Esq. Metcalf."[55] After seizing the men, they left a message with Pomeroy's wife, stating that the men were hostages "to secure the life of Jason Parmenter and Henry McCullock, who are condemned to death by the State." The note went on to promise that if Parmenter and McCullough were executed, their hostages "shall be put to death, in the same manner, as soon as the news arrives."[56] In early June, five or six armed men burst into a home in Great Barrington at midnight, where they proceeded to threaten a man inside. One of the intruders turned to another and asked if he should shoot the man. The other intruder replied, "No, we will first strip, and then kill him." They took off the man's shirt, "and then ordered his Britches off (the only cover he had on)." Seeing this, the man's mother "went into fitts," and when the men turned to tell her that "they would stop her Damnd noise," the man jumped out the window as escaped. The men then left the house before proceeding to threaten other townspeople and rob several homes, including the home of the minister.[57] A similar attack took place in the Lanesborough on June 13, when several men burst into a home late at night bearing guns with bayonets fixed, and they threatened the residents before making off with clothing and other personal goods.[58]

As soon as the death sentences were handed down, petitions for clemency for all of the convicted men began to be sent to Boston. Petitions came not only from friends and family and others sympathetic to the insurgents but also from many staunch supporters of government who earlier had called for swift and vigorous punishments. For example, the first petitions in support of Henry Gale of Princeton came from his wife, Betty.[59] But Henry also received considerable support from many of his neighbors in Princeton, including some of the leading figures in the town, who noted that they "have been on the side of Government in the late unhappy tumults, and some of them have Risqued their lives in defense of the Constitution," but that they felt very concerned regarding "the Distresses of the Convicts family." The petitioners acknowledged that Gale appeared to have played a prominent role in some of the disturbances in the fall—he was identified as a leader of the group of armed men who closed the court at Worcester on September 5— but, as one petition put it, "when the popular Clamour had in some degree subsided and he had time to recollect himself, he came to a full Determination (as we believe) to Return to the Duty of his Allegiance."[60] Another petition was signed by more than sixty townspeople—who also stressed that they were "no Friends to Rebellion"—and also pleaded for clemency for Gale because they believed that he had "repented."[61] A final document in support of Gale was a deposition from Captain Boas Moore of Princeton, who stated that he talked with Gale on January 30, 1787, a day after Gale had returned to Princeton. Boas related that Gale said "he meant to Keep about his Business at Home" and that he now "Disapproved the Conduct of the Insurgents."[62] Moore related that on that day he told Gale that the insurgents were interested in radical change and that Gale replied that "it was not his Aim to Distroy the Constitution but to obtain redress of some Grievances."[63]

Like those for Henry Gale, the petitions for Henry McCullough of Pelham also stressed that, while he was guilty of taking part in the insurgency, he was a young man who was unduly influenced by others in the community. The people of Pelham fully supported McCullough, and as Justice Ebenezer Matoon explained it, a pardon for McCullough would be a powerful way to reconnect the people of Pelham to government, while his execution would have the opposite effect: "If he is spared the town of Pelham is attached to government, if he is executed . . . the affections of the town is lost."[64] In addition to trying to reaffirm loyalty, others emphasized that the men who were sentenced to death were not the men who led the insurgency in January and

February. Even Theodore Sedgwick, whose law office had been broken into on the morning of February 25, wrote on behalf of Peter Wilcox, who had been arrested following the armed conflict near Sheffield later that same day. Sedgwick argued that the men most deserving of capital punishment were not in custody: "From an unfortunate combination of circumstances, it has so happened that those who were the most proper objects of capital punishment are now beyond the reach of Justice." Sedgwick went on to say that Wilcox had behaved well since his arrest, and he had received many character references. Finally, Sedgwick even tried to explain away the prominent role Wilcox played on the evening of February 25. "It is said, however, that during the action he manifested a degree of bravery superior to his Fellows." For Sedgwick, that was not a problem: "A cowardly traitor to me is the most detestable of all characters. Such as one may do mischief in a bad, but can never be of service to a good cause."[65] Governor Bowdoin and his council began meeting on April 27 to consider the men facing a death sentence, and while they pardoned several, they set the execution dates for the others. In Berkshire County, Peter Wilcox and Nathaniel Austin were to be executed on May 21, as were Henry McCullough and Jason Parmenter in Hampshire, and Henry Gale in Worcester. Job Shattuck, who had been held in jail in Boston since late November, was scheduled to die on May 28. Once the execution dates were set, more petitions arrived on behalf of the condemned men, and the council reprieved their death sentence until June 21.

Meanwhile, the legislature gathered in late May to consider the election results that had been sent in from the towns. The results were stunning. Voter turnout expanded dramatically, and for the first time in state history an incumbent governor was defeated: John Hancock defeated Bowdoin by winning 75 percent of the vote. In both the Senate and House elections, many incumbents were defeated and replaced by political newcomers. In the forty-member Senate, only twelve incumbents won reelection, while in the House, many towns that had not bothered to send representatives in recent years did so in 1787.[66] In 1786 only 193 representatives were present when the legislature first met, but in 1787 the number mushroomed to 262.[67]

The dramatic turnover in government did represent a strong critique of the government's handling of the regulator movement, but it was far from a takeover by the forces of regulation. In fact, three men accused of ties with the regulators were not allowed to take their seats in the House of Representatives. Some reform legislation was passed: all pardoned men had their civil rights restored, and no new direct taxes were authorized. But as in the previous session, a proposal for paper money was soundly rejected. Like the new legislature, Governor Hancock did not radically depart from the policies of his predecessor, although he did offer a change in tone. Unlike Bowdoin, who had vetoed a legislative effort to reduce his own salary, Hancock willingly accepted the same salary reduction that Bowdoin had refused. In many ways, however, Hancock's policies had much in common with Bowdoin's. One of the first things Hancock did as governor was to ask for an additional five hundred to eight hundred troops to be stationed in the western part of the state. Hancock's other primary concern was with the fate of the condemned men. He had officially replaced Bowdoin on June 2, less than three weeks before June 21, when the first executions were scheduled. He began meeting with his council, and they decided on June 16 that the executions should be postponed until August 2 in order to see if any new violence would erupt. As part of their plan, they directed that their reprieve not be made public until the last possible minute. In other words, the hangman was to go through all the preparations, even to the point of bringing the men to the gallows. Then, and only then, was the sheriff to announce that their execution had been postponed.[68]

The two men scheduled to die in Hampshire County were Jason Parmenter and Henry McCullough. On the morning of June 21, they were led from the Northampton jail by sheriff Elisha Porter and escorted by four hundred members of the militia to the meetinghouse, where Rev. Baldwin of Palmer preached a sermon. The men were then brought to the gallows, where their death warrants were read by the sheriff; according to the *Worcester Magazine*, "Every preparation was made, as if they were really to have been executed; even their coffins were carried with them to the gallows." Then, right before they were to be hanged, the sheriff read their reprieve, which stated that their date of execution had been delayed to August 2. A large crowd had gathered to witness the execution, and while there were different responses to news of the reprieve, there was no effort on the part of the crowd to rescue McCullough and Parmenter, who were both brought back to the jail.[69]

A similar drama unfolded for Henry Gale, who faced execution in the town of Worcester. Before the date of Gale's execution, there were some calls for the hanging to take place as scheduled, while others called for a full pardon, but *Worcester Magazine* editor Isaiah Thomas supported the decision for a temporary reprieve. According to Thomas, if government officials had gone through with the execution, then they might have been seen as engaging in "an act of revenge," which would have been met with strong disapproval in the western part of the state, especially because "nearly all the men who had supported government in the western counties, have become petitioners" in favor of the condemned. If the men had been fully pardoned, though, it might be interpreted as a sign of weakness on the part of government. The fact that the government could go through the motions of an execution without following through showed that they had the authority but chose not to exercise it. More importantly, the government had it in its power to execute men if violence returned to the state. In effect, the reprieves were a way for the government to hold the condemned men hostage in order to prevent any new efforts at armed resistance or retribution.[70]

In Great Barrington in Berkshire County, Peter Wilcox and Nathaniel Austin had faced the same situation as Parmenter, McCullough, and Gale. Back in May, before the first reprieve, both the men and their wives sent petitions to the governor and his council for mercy. Like most of the other condemned men, Wilcox and Austin pleaded for their lives because they said they recognized and regretted the mistakes they had made. They also emphasized that, if executed, they would both leave behind a widow and young children. Their wives, Humillis Austin and Molly Wilcox, implored the authorities to spare their husbands for their children's sake: "Will you suffer our Little Infants to be Fatherless and doom them to pass through the Journey of Life, Children of Misfortune, subject to a Thousand Reproaches from the unfeeling and ungenerous: Surely Not!"[71] Both the wives' petition and the petition of the condemned men concluded by requesting a delay in the proceedings, even if government officials did eventually plan on going through with the executions. They told the governor that they wanted the delay so that "By Repentance and faith," the men might be able to gain "an interest in that Glorious Redemption which was purchased by our Lord & Saviour with his most precious Blood for a Guilty World!"[72] While in the Great Barrington jail, Austin and Wilcox did more than pray for salvation. On the evening of June 15—the night before governor and council stayed their execution until August—Austin and Wilcox were being guarded by a young man by the name of Abel Holman. Holman, who had volunteered to serve in the government militia, had been given the task of watching the prisoners. Unfortunately for Holman, that night Austin and Wilcox had a visitor or visitors who brought along some alcohol.[73] Holman—who later described himself as "young and inconsiderate, and much fatigued with his task"—was offered some of their "spiritous liquor," and he accepted. Once the young guard was drunk, the two men escaped the jail with the help of a "young woman."[74]

As a halfhearted search began for Austin and Wilcox, the council debated the fate of Job Shattuck. Shattuck was considered the most prominent regulator in custody, and in the days leading up to his scheduled execution at the end of June the council at first refused to entertain a reprieve for Shattuck. Only a request from one member of the council to reconsider Shattuck's case two days before the execution led to another discussion and a reprieve until July 26.[75] Another long debate in July led to a reprieve until September 20, and on September 12 the council granted a full pardon to the four men still in jail. In the fall, the state Supreme Judicial Court tried and sentenced four other men to death. One, William Manning, had played a role in the armed conflict outside Sheffield on February 25. His sentence was later reduced to a seven-year prison term at the Castle Island prison in Boston Harbor. The other three men were convicted of breaking into Berkshire County homes in May and June and do not appear to have played a major role in the earlier regulator movement. While one of the robbers was pardoned, the other two men, both described in newspaper accounts as "laborers," were hanged in Lenox on December 6, 1787.

While officials in Vermont and New York took measures in the late spring and summer to prevent meetings of insurgent groups, there was not a massive effort to locate and capture regulator leaders. In January 1788, Luke Day was captured by some New Hampshire residents interested in the £100 reward. Day was charged, but his case never came to trial, and he was eventually released. In February 1788, Daniel Shays and Eli Parsons petitioned the legislature for a pardon.[76] In their petition, both men pledged their loyalty to the state and asked for forgiveness for actions that they said they realized "cannot be justified." They told the legislature that if they wanted to continue to have them suffer as an example "to prevent similar disorders," the men said that "there is scarcely an inconvenience or misfortune, to which they had not already been exposed." They had been forced to flee their homes, live in fear of capture, and travel "far from friends and connections in a state of exile." In addition, Shays and Parsons reminded the legislators that if they were granted a pardon, it would ensure that they and their "friends, wives, and children, who are innocent," would be "ever bound by new ties of gratitude and affection . . . to the government." In the summer of 1788, with the threat of armed resistance neutralized, the Massachusetts legislature agreed, and Shays and Parsons both received a pardon.[77]

# Shays's Rebellion and the Constitution

By THE SPRING of 1787, the conflict now commonly known as Shays's Rebellion was essentially over. For those who played a direct role as either a regulator or a "friend of government," the results were often significant. Only a few men were killed or physically injured, but many regulators, including Daniel Shays, abandoned their homes and never returned. Others, like Governor Bowdoin, suffered political defeat, while militia General William Shepard would always face local popular derision for his decision to fire upon the regulators in order to protect the federal armory. Beyond the impact on the principal actors, however, what was the broader significance of the conflict? For one thing, it highlighted the fact that a state like Massachusetts, which in many ways was relatively homogeneous in terms of ethnicity, religious belief, and language, could still be deeply divided by different economic and political cultures. The conflict also raised critical questions about the rights and responsibilities of citizens who found certain government policies oppressive, as well as the proper response of government authorities who were not only responsible for maintaining order but who were also cognizant that the people's identification with and loyalty to that fledgling government were not automatic but would need to be cultivated.

Writing at the end of the 1790s, Massachusetts farmer William Manning drew several lessons from the events of 1786 and 1787. During the rebellion, Manning was sympathetic to those who were critical of government, and he agreed that the distress in the Massachusetts countryside was genuine, but he had been opposed to measures to forcibly close the courts. On the one hand, Manning believed that Governor Bowdoin's defeat amid unprecedentedly high voter turnout in the election of 1787 was a vindication of republican forms of government: "This is a streiking demonstration of the advantages of a free elective government, & shews how a peopel may run themselves into the gratest diffilcultyes by inatention in elections & retreve their circumstances again by attending theirtoo." On the other hand, Manning believed that the rebellion "neaver would have hapned if the peopel had bin posesed of a true knowledge of their Rights, Dutyes, & Interests." For Manning, the way to prevent powerful political figures (such as Governor Bowdoin) from abusing their power was to ensure that the electorate at large had a clear knowledge of current political events and acted on that knowledge by communicating with each other and by fully participating in all elections. The direct and often contentious local mobilization of county conventions and armed crowds that had been essential to the revolution should give way to formal electoral politics.[1]

While William Manning observed Shays's Rebellion from the town of North Billerica in Massachusetts, Thomas Jefferson was living in Paris at the time of the uprising. Jefferson shared Manning's view that the way to prevent the abuse of power was to have an educated and engaged electorate: "Were it left to me to decide whether we should have a government without newspapers, or newspapers without a government, I should not hesitate a moment to prefer the latter. But I should mean that every man should receive those papers, and be capable of reading them."[2] But Jefferson went farther than Manning in arguing that government authorities should be lenient with any men who engaged in rebellion. For Jefferson, acts of rebellion against a republic were wrong, but because the people themselves were the ultimate safeguard of their liberty (which according to classical republican theory was always threatened by government power), they should not be punished severely. In fact, in a letter to James Madison dated January 30, 1787, Jefferson said that "I hold it that a little rebellion now and then is a good thing, and as necessary in the political world as storms in the physical . . . It is a medicine necessary for the sound health of government."[3] Jefferson admitted that allowing such actions to take place would make society more turbulent, but it would also make it more likely that liberties and rights would be protected. As Jefferson put it in a letter to Abigail Adams, "The spirit of resistance to government is so valuable on certain occasions, that I wish it to be always kept alive. It will often be exercised when wrong, but better so than not to be exercised at all."[4]

In most ways, the response of Massachusetts authorities ultimately matched Jefferson's prescription of mild punishment, even if the initial government reaction was more stern. At first, the legislature tried to exact retribution by prosecuting any regulator leaders it could capture and by excluding most regulators from the body politic for a period of three years, but such exclusionary efforts were rejected by authorities like Benjamin Lincoln and by the voters in the state elections in the spring of 1787. Most regulators—including putative leaders like Daniel Shays and Job Shattuck—were pardoned after they made efforts to reestablish their loyalty to government. Despite such an ultimately mild response, there was a significant number of powerful Americans who did not share the views of Manning or Jefferson toward the rebellion. Their response to the Massachusetts regulation of 1786–87 would help shape the framing and ratification of the United States Constitution.

On September 12, 1786—the same day that regulators forced the adjournment of courts in Bristol, Middlesex, and Berkshire counties—representatives from five states had gathered for a second day of meetings in Annapolis, Maryland. The Annapolis Convention had been called by members of the Confederation Congress who wanted to discuss the possibility of amending the Articles of Confederation to give the national Congress the authority to regulate trade and commerce. Ever since 1781, there had been efforts to give the federal government more power to tax and shape trade policy, but all previous efforts to amend the articles had been unable to achieve the required unanimous consent of all thirteen states. Not much was likely to come of the Annapolis meeting either, as the delegations from four states were late in arriving, and four other states did not bother to send any delegates at all. Those who were present, however, decided to recommend that another meeting take place in Philadelphia the following May in order to propose changes to the articles, and they requested that states send representatives to that spring convention.

## The Decision to Attend the Philadelphia Convention

By the fall of 1786, many political figures in Massachusetts were becoming increasingly concerned with the inability of the central government to raise revenue and to regulate, support, and defend transatlantic trade. Despite this concern, there was also a reluctance on the part of many to play a role in the Annapolis Convention for fear that any changes to the Articles of Confederation might give southern states more authority and control in a revised national government.[5] Massachusetts had selected representatives for Annapolis, but most of the men chosen refused to attend, and by the time the replacements assembled and set off for Annapolis, they were too late to make the meeting.[6]

Over the course of the fall and winter, as the conflict unfolded and the regulation was suppressed, more and more prominent Massachusetts politicians came to believe that a stronger national government was needed to prevent future conflicts. They did so for two reasons: first, the insurgency disrupted tax collection so dramatically that government income from tax receipts basically stopped between the fall of 1786 and the spring of 1787. Without that income, the state could not make its interest payments to its creditors, and with future payments in doubt, the market value of these securities fell. Over time, holders of public state securities could see that they would be better off if a stronger federal government (with the power to tax) assumed that debt and would be better able to pay this interest.[7] Second, the insurgency itself made some prominent politicians come to believe that a stronger central government would be needed to maintain social order and protect property. After the first round of court closures in August and September 1786, Rufus King wrote that "the great Body of the people are, without Virtue, and not governed by any internal restraints of Conscience."[8] Elbridge Gerry, a member of the Massachusetts legislature who had long been suspicious of power concentrated in the hands of an aristocratic few, was influenced by the rebellion to become more sensitive to the possibility that mobs could also serve as a tyrannical force. While Gerry would ultimately come to oppose the Constitution, his experience during the rebellion led him to serve as one of Massachusetts's delegates to the Philadelphia Convention, and in his first speech he advocated a stronger central government to prevent the "anarchy as now exists."[9] One of the biggest champions of a stronger central government, Henry Knox, told George Washington in late December, that the "commotions of Massachusetts" had made many men come to believe that without a stronger central government "there is no hope for liberty and property."[10] The actions of the regulators generated such calls for a stronger government that Mercy Otis Warren, who later wrote a three-volume history of the American Revolution, believed that some conservatives were working behind the scenes to instigate a rebellion that would convince others that a stronger central government was needed.[11]

Conspiracy or no, word of the conflict in Massachusetts spread far and wide, and many supporters of a stronger central government interpreted the conflict as clear evidence that significant reform of the Articles of Confederation was necessary. For example, from his home in Mount Vernon, Virginia, George Washington was paying close attention to the events in Massachusetts. Virginia was one of the first states to endorse the Philadelphia convention, and by December 4, 1786, Virginia governor Edmund Randolph had chosen Washington to be one of the delegates who would represent the commonwealth in Philadelphia. Since the end of the Revolutionary War, Washington had been retired from politics, and he had been supervising his sprawling plantation enterprise. Washington had long believed that a stronger central government was needed, and he hoped that the meeting in Philadelphia might advance that cause, but when he received the news from Governor Randolph that he had been chosen to serve as one of Virginia's representatives, he at first politely declined. He had already turned down an offer to attend the Society of Cincinnati meeting scheduled for Philadelphia at the same time as the proposed convention. He had not wanted to attend because of the controversy surrounding the society's decision to allow local chapters to maintain a policy of only admitting Revolutionary War officers and their firstborn male descendants. Washington also feared how it might look for him to return to politics after his public retirement from the army (which had won him so much praise). Washington also enjoyed life at Mount Vernon and did not relish engaging once again in a public career. After receiving his letter, Governor Randolph decided not to accept Washington's refusal, telling him instead that he would reserve the position for him if and when he chose to accept. Supporters of a stronger central government like Randolph recognized that if Washington attended the convention, it would add to its legitimacy and potential importance.

Meanwhile, Washington had been receiving letters from former aides David Humphreys and Henry Knox describing the growing crisis in Massachusetts. Washington became extremely concerned, and he asked his friends to help him understand what was behind the conflict: "Does it proceed from licentiousness, British-influence disseminated by Tories, or real grievances which admit of redress?"[12] Back in October, Henry Knox was the first to make Washington aware of what was happening in Massachusetts. Knox dismissed the claims of people who said that taxes were too high. The cause, Knox said, was that the poor majority was jealous of the rich minority: "They feel at once their own poverty, compared with the opulent, and their own force, and they are determined to make use of the latter, in order to remedy the former." Knox told Washington that the angry western farmers were interested in a redistribution of wealth: "Their creed is 'That the property of the United States has been protected from the confiscations of Britain by the joint exertions of all, and therefore ought to be the common property of all. And he that attempts opposition to this creed is an enemy to equity and justice, and ought to be swept from off the face of the earth.'" For Knox, this could be accomplished through a program of paper money, debt relief, and tender laws: "They are determined to annihilate all debts public and private and have agrarian Laws which are easily effected by the means of unfunded paper money which shall be a tender in all cases whatever." Knox informed Washington that he thought that about 20 percent of the people in some counties in Massachusetts supported such proposals, and if they joined with like-minded people in other New England states, they could create a force of "12 or 15000 desperate & unprincipled men."

Knox went on to tell Washington that the American republic had been created by people who valued liberty, and they had believed that people would be virtuous enough so that society would be orderly without the need for too much coercion. For Knox, such a vision was naive, as the events in Massachusetts were indicating: "We imagined that the mildness of our government and the virtue of the people were so correspondent, that we were not as other nations requiring brutal force to support the laws—But we find that we are men, actual men, possessing all the turbulent passions belonging to that animal and that we must have a government proper and adequate to him."[13] Knox followed with two more letters in December, adding that he worried that a large insurgent force would get help from the British in Canada, and Knox's portrayal of the regulators was persuasive to Washington. Washington replied to Knox by telling him that the insurgents were probably already receiving assistance from the British, and he feared that the sentiments of the Massachusetts insurgents had the potential to spread not just through New England but throughout all of the states.[14] After the reports from Knox, Washington began to tell other prominent political figures what the conflict in Massachusetts signified. In a letter to James Madison in early November, Washington feared that the conflict in Massachusetts was evidence that government authority was too weak to survive. Instead of regulators who carefully chose limited targets, Washington envisioned uncontrollable mobs: "What stronger evidence can be given of the want of energy in our governments than these disorders? If there exists not a power to check them, what security has a man of life, liberty, or property?" For Washington, the overarching lesson was a recognition that the current system had to be fundamentally altered: "Thirteen Sovereignties pulling against each other, and all tugging at the fœderal head, will soon bring ruin on the whole; whereas a liberal, and energetic Constitution, well guarded & closely watched, to prevent incroachments, might restore us to that degree of respectability & consequence, to which we had a fair claim, & the brightest prospect of attaining."[15]

Washington did not agree to represent Virginia in Philadelphia until the spring of 1787, after the insurgency in Massachusetts had been defeated, and other factors no doubt shaped his decision to attend. But the fact that such a conflict had happened in Massachusetts suggested to Washington that it could happen anywhere. As he wrote to the Marquis de Lafayette at the end of March, the events in Massachusetts were "evident marks of a defective government; indeed the thinking part of the people of this Country are now so well satisfied of this fact that most of the Legislatures have appointed" delegates to the Philadelphia convention.[16] The events in Massachusetts were the most violent manifestation of a conflict that had emerged to some degree in every state in the union. Every state was laboring to pay off its own debts, as well as its share of the federal debt. Strident calls for debt and tax relief had led to the authorization of paper money in four states and protests in others.[17] Many supporters of a stronger national government now converged on Philadelphia hopeful that they could create a new framework of government more insulated from popular pressure.

By the time the delegates gathered in Philadelphia in May, the conflict in Massachusetts was coming to an end, and on only a handful of occasions did delegates speak of the Massachusetts regulators. But in at least a couple of ways that conflict impacted the shape of the Constitution itself. One of the main criticisms of the Articles of Confederation is that it did not provide any

Detail of a print depicting the political situation in Connecticut on the eve of the ratification of the U.S. Constitution. The men shown here are the Anti-federalist faction on Connecticut's Governor's Council. They call for a tax on luxury, note that the "people are oprest," curse the federal government, and wish "Success to Shays." The artist, who supports the Constitution, has these men trying to pull the state toward storms and fire, while the Federalist faction (not pictured here) is trying to pull the state toward a sunny future. On January 8, 1788, Connecticut became the fifth state to ratify the Constitution. Source: "The looking glass for 1787. A house divided against itself cannot stand. Mat. chap. 13th verse 26." This image is a detail from a larger image available from the Library of Congress website, http://www.loc.gov/pictures/item/2008661778/.

clear way for the federal government to respond to insurrections or other disorders within the states. While Secretary of War Henry Knox had been instrumental in getting the Confederation Congress to authorize more than thirteen hundred troops in the fall of 1786, only a fraction of that force was ever assembled, largely because funds to support the force were not forthcoming from the states. By contrast, the framers of the Constitution gave the federal government the authority to raise money directly to fund an army, and in emergencies it could take over state militias.[18] In addition to giving the federal government a greater ability to raise military forces, framers of the Constitution also were motivated by the belief that state legislatures had been unable to effectively prevent debtors from passing relief legislation like paper currency and personal property tender laws to the detriment of creditors. In Massachusetts, the legislature's staunch opposition to such relief legislation—combined with its efforts to levy and rigorously collect taxes—had been among the primary reasons why the regulators began to protest in the first place. And while the regulation was repressed, spring elections in 1787 had led to some relief legislation in the state. In response, the document framed in Philadelphia would take away the states' ability to issue paper money and pass tender laws.[19]

## The Ratification Debate in Massachusetts

On September 28, 1787, the Confederation Congress released the Constitution to the states for ratification. According to the Congress, nine of the thirteen states would need to approve or ratify the Constitution for it to become the new framework of government. In Massachusetts, the state legislature called on the state's 298 towns to select representatives to a constitutional convention that would take place in Boston in January. Accordingly, towns throughout the state met over the next two months to choose delegates. In some towns, the meetings became quite contentious. For example, in Great Barrington, a protracted meeting on November 26 led to the selection of a candidate opposed to the Constitution along with a committee report recommending a list of instructions for the delegate. The instructions identified objections to the Constitution, and one of the instructions called for delegates to insist on a roll call of votes: "that the world may know who are friends to the Liberties of this Commonwealth and who not." After more debate, the town meeting was adjourned for a week, and when it reconvened, an even larger group ultimately voted down the committee's instructions 55 to 51, and the previous week's delegate selection was reconsidered. A new vote was held, and now the candidate who expressed support for the Constitution narrowly won the vote.[20] In other towns with less internal conflict, there was nevertheless a great deal of interest, discussion, and debate.

When the Massachusetts state convention began on January 9, 1788, there was a total of 364 delegates representing 272 towns, which was a dramatic increase over recent representation in the legislature. Ninety-nine towns that had not been represented in 1786 would be represented at the Constitutional

Convention,[21] and most of these towns were from either the settlements in Maine or the central and western counties of Worcester, Hampshire, and Berkshire. When the convention opened, many supporters of the Constitution were worried that the high turnout would work against them. In addition, there were men associated with the regulator movement who had been chosen by their towns as delegates. The town of Rehoboth in Bristol County sent Phanuel Bishop, who had been refused a senate seat the previous year for his support of the regulators. Nine men who had been included on Attorney General Paine's "Black List" of prominent regulators were chosen by their towns, including Benjamin Ely of West Springfield.[22] According to supporter of the government Henry Jackson, "The whole opposition, in this commonwealth, is that cursed spirit of insurgency that prevailed last winter."[23] Jackson's statement was an exaggeration, because there was a significant number of delegates who had opposed the regulation but who had doubts about the Constitution. But the evidence seems clear that dozens of towns sent delegates who had either played a role in the regulation or were sympathetic to it, and such men were an important part of the opposition to ratification.[24] Writing to George Washington, Benjamin Lincoln was concerned about the prospects of passage: "We find ourselves exceedingly embarrassed by the temper which raged the last winter in some of the counties. Many of the insurgents are in the Convention; even some of Shays's officers. A great proportion of these men are high in the opposition."[25]

By the time the Massachusetts convention convened on January 9, 1788, no one could predict how much support ratification had, and most observers believed that it was likely to be a very close vote. At that point, five states had already voted for the constitution, but Massachusetts would be the first convention held in a state where opinion over the Constitution was so sharply divided. Once the convention began meeting, a decision was made that each paragraph of the Constitution would be debated in order, but no votes would be taken until the entire debate had taken place. This rule allowed supporters of the Constitution to respond to criticisms as they emerged. Many prominent politicians and most lawyers and college graduates supported the Constitution, and they were able to employ their public-speaking abilities and confidence to make persuasive arguments on behalf of the Constitution. After several weeks of debate, a critic of the Constitution, sixty-seven-year-old Amos Singletary of Sutton, rose to voice his concerns. Singletary had long been critical of government power, and he had been a prominent figure in organizing county conventions since 1781. In January 1787, in the critical days leading up to the march of Benjamin Lincoln's army, Singletary had been one of the men who had unsuccessfully pleaded with the Governor's Council to recall the militia.[26] Now, Singletary believed that the supporters of the Constitution were conning simple people into giving up their liberties: "These lawyers, and men of learning, and moneyed men, that talk so finely, and gloss over matters so smoothly, to make us, poor illiterate people, swallow down the pill." Once that happened, Singletary warned, they would take control of government "and get all the power and all the money into their own hands, and then swallow up all of us little folks, like the great leviathan . . . swallowed up Jonah."[27]

In a response to Singletary, the delegate from the town of Lanesborough in Berkshire county, Jonathan Smith, rose to address the convention. Smith identified himself as a farmer, a "plain man" who was not used to speaking in public. He told the convention that his community had recently come to recognize "the worth of good government by the want of it." Smith said that back in 1786 "There was a black cloud that rose in the east . . . and spread over the west." Another delegate interrupted and asked him what he meant by the east. Smith responded that it began in Bristol County, which was the first county to hold a convention in the summer of 1786. Smith said that the movement had led to anarchy, which would inevitably lead to tyranny: "People that used to live peaceably, and were before good neighbours, got distracted and took up arms against government." Smith was again interrupted, as someone who hoped to get Smith's speech ruled out of order asked what these events had to do with the Constitution. Smith was allowed to continue, and he said that he would show "the effects of anarchy, that you may see the reasons why I wish for good government." Smith then went on to describe the events that took place in Berkshire after the regulators had been stopped in Springfield and flushed from Petersham. He said that insurgents would "rob you of your property, threaten to burn your houses; oblige you to be on your guard night and day." Smith described the armed conflict that took place in Sheffield on February 25, 1787, when "poor prisoners were set in the front, to be killed by their own friends." He said that this violence was so devastating that "had any person, that was able to protect us, come and set up his standard we should all have flocked to it, even if it had been a monarch, and that monarch may have proved a tyrant."[28]

It is impossible to know what impact Smith's words had on the assembled audience, or if his argument helped sway anyone to support ratification. In 1786 and 1787, regulators and their sympathizers had railed against a state government that seemed indifferent to their troubles and bent on protecting the interests of creditors and government officials. The Constitution would create a more distant federal government with potentially even more power, and with less local input. It is clear that most of those men who arrived prepared to vote against the Constitution were not swayed. When the final vote was taken on February 6, only seven of Berkshire County's twenty-two delegates voted for the Constitution. In Hampshire County, which was home to many market-oriented towns in the Connecticut River valley, thirty-three delegates supported and nineteen opposed, while in Worcester County forty-two delegates joined Amos Singletary to vote no, while only seven voted to ratify. A majority of Middlesex and Bristol County delegates also voted against the Constitution. But enough supporters in these towns joined the vast majority of delegates in coastal counties to lead to a final vote of 187 delegates in support, and 168 against. Most historians agree that the supporters of the Constitution were able to prevail because they offered to recommend amendments to the Constitution after a vote of approval (rather than considering the amendments as a prerequisite to ratification). In addition, the appearance of an ailing and previously ambivalent John Hancock toward the end of the convention probably swayed some voters when the popular governor voiced his support for ratification.[29]

After ratification in Massachusetts, conventions would ratify the Constitution in five more states by July, and within another year the Constitution would go into effect. In Massachusetts, most of the men who voted against the constitution did pledge to support the new framework of government, although a group of critics maintained its public opposition after the vote.[30] Much of that criticism vanished after the ratification of the Bill of Rights in 1791. Meanwhile, the Massachusetts economy improved as European crop failures and political conflict opened up markets for the products of American farms. In addition, because the federal government had the power to raise revenue directly, Massachusetts no longer needed to try and impose high direct taxes. Instead, the federal government relied predominantly on taxes on imports, which greatly reduced the tax burden on Massachusetts farm communities. As secretary of the treasury, Alexander Hamilton devised a plan for the federal government to take on (or "assume") the remaining wartime state debt, which won the support of creditors. His plan to fund this consolidated debt included levying an excise tax on whiskey, which aggravated farmers in western Pennsylvania, who fought back by employing many of the same methods used by the Massachusetts regulators. President Washington responded by using the powers allowed under the Constitution to raise an army of thirteen thousand that he personally led to put down the rebellion.

# Acknowledgments

The impetus for this book began when I started teaching early American history at Merrimack College in Massachusetts. I went to graduate school in the Midwest and wrote a dissertation on the post-Revolutionary Chesapeake, but after my move to Merrimack I wanted to be able to provide my predominantly New England–born students with more local detail and examples. I want to thank the students in my Revolutionary America course with providing feedback to some early versions of the narrative.

I am grateful to the Massachusetts Historical Society for granting permission to quote from its Shays' Rebellion and Benjamin Lincoln papers. I received helpful and cheerful assistance there, as well as at the American Antiquarian Society and the Massachusetts State Archives in Boston.

A number of people offered timely assistance that made this book possible. At Merrimack, Vice Provost Cindy McGowan was able to help me secure a sabbatical after it looked like I might have to wait another year, and my department colleague Susan Vorderer graciously agreed to step in and serve as department chair while I was away. While on sabbatical, I was able to work close to home in the library at First Church in Nashua, New Hampshire. I want to thank Rev. James Chaloner for making the space available as well as Sue Englander and Pam Hickey for making my stay comfortable and productive.

I also would like to thank my sister, Colleen Condon, who provided essential early encouragement as well as very helpful technical advice as I navigated the complicated terrain of both geographic information system and illustration software to make the maps included in the book. Early on, my mother Rose Marie Condon helped kindle my love of history with lots of books and trips to places like Washington, D.C., and she has always supported me, even if she privately wondered if my many years of school were entirely necessary.

The book benefited greatly from anonymous reader reports, copyediting from Brian MacDonald, feedback from series editor Peter C. Hoffer, and guidance from general editor Bob Brugger.

I want to thank my children, Leo and Flannery, for providing me with daily examples of resistance to authority, and I want to thank my wife, Liz Dols, for everything else.

# Notes

PROLOGUE: Worcester, Massachusetts, September 5–6, 1786

1. September 5 Narrative of a Riot in the county of Worcester Transmitted to the Governor by Artemas Ward, Massachusetts Archives (hereafter MA) v. 190: 231–32, Massachusetts State Archives, Boston; Robert A. Feer, *Shays's Rebellion* (New York: Garland, 1988), 185–95.

2. MA v. 190: 231–32.

3. *Dictionary of American Biography*, ed. Dumas Malone (New York: Scribner, 1936), 19:415–16.

4. MA v. 190: 231–33; Some historical accounts maintain that Ward's speech lasted for two hours. For several reasons why it likely did not last that long, see Feer, *Shays's Rebellion*, 191–93.

5. Sheriff Greenleaf to Governor Bowdoin, MA v. 190: 235.

6. Leonard L. Richards, *Shays's Rebellion: The American Revolution's Final Battle* (Philadelphia: University of Pennsylvania Press, 2002), 111.

7. *Worcester Magazine*, fourth week, November 1786, v. II, 414.

8. Jonathan Warner to Governor Bowdoin, MA v. 190: 230.

9. MA v. 190: 233.

10. Ibid.

11. Ray Raphael, *The First American Revolution: Before Lexington and Concord* (New York: New Press, 2002), 130–38.

CHAPTER ONE: Paying for Independence

1. Robert J. Taylor, ed., *Massachusetts, Colony to Commonwealth: Documents on the Formation of Its Constitution, 1775–1780* (Chapel Hill: University of North Carolina Press, 1961), 19.

2. Stephen E. Patterson, *Political Parties in Revolutionary Massachusetts* (Madison: University of Wisconsin Press, 1973), 219–27.

3. Ibid., 230.

4. Ibid., 432–33.

5. Oscar Handlin and Mary F. Handlin, eds., *The Popular Sources of Political Authority: Documents on the Massachusetts Constitution of 1780* (Cambridge, MA: Belknap Press of Harvard University Press, 1966), 596.

6. Patterson, *Political Parties*, 244–46.

7. Ibid., 160.

8. Joseph Plumb Martin, *A Narrative of Some of the Adventures, Dangers and Sufferings of a Revolutionary Soldier* (New York: Little, Brown, 1962), 287.

9. E. James Ferguson, *The Power of the Purse: A History of American Public Finance, 1776–1790* (Chapel Hill: University of North Carolina Press, 1961), 50–53.

10. Act passed May 5, 1780, can be found in *The Acts and Resolves Public and Private of the Province of the Massachusetts Bay* (Boston, 1886), 5:1178–83.

11. "Aminidab" in *Massachusetts Spy* (Worcester), March 22, 1781.

12. *Boston Gazette*, May 14, 1781.

13. Van Beck Hall, *Politics Without Parties: Massachusetts, 1780–1791* (Pittsburgh: University of Pittsburgh Press, 1972), 106–8; vote percentages in table 27, 102–3.

14. "Aminidab" in *Massachusetts Spy* (Worcester), March 22, 1781.

15. Ibid.

16. "Sydney" in *Massachusetts Spy* (Worcester), March 1, 1781.

17. *Acts and Resolves of Massachusetts, 1780–81* (Boston, 1890), 314, https://archive .org/details/actsresolvespass178081mass.

18. Hall, *Politics Without Parties*, 110–11.

19. "An Act for Apportioning and Assessing a Tax of Two Hundred Thousand Pounds" (Boston: Benjamin Edes and Sons, 1782), in *Early American Imprints, Series 1, Evans*, no. 44217.

20. Roger H. Brown, *Redeeming the Republic: Federalists, Taxation, and the Origins of the Constitution* (Baltimore: Johns Hopkins University Press, 1993), 247–48.

21. "An Act, For Apportioning and Assessing a Tax of [£374,785]" (Boston: Benjamin Edes & Sons, 1781), in *Early American Imprints, Series 1, Evans*, no. 17224.

22. Roger Brown, *Redeeming the Republic*, 98.

23. Ibid.

24. Petition from Collectors of Taxes in the town of Berwick for the year 1781, May 29, 1783, Massachusetts Archives (hereafter MA) v. 188: 314, Massachusetts State Archives, Boston.

25. "An Act for Apportioning and Assessing a Tax of [£303,634]" (Boston: Benjamin Edes & Sons, 1781), in *Early American Imprints, Series 1, Evans*, no. 17225.

26. Deposition of Esack Sprague (Pittsfield, Jan 22, 1783, nine o'clock at night), MA v. 154: 366; this episode is also described by Robert A. Feer, *Shays's Rebellion* (New York: Garland, 1988), 167–69.

27. MA v. 154: 366.

28. Ibid.

29. Deposition of Chaney Ensign, MA v. 154: 358.

30. Deposition of Ebenezer Squire, MA v. 154: 161.

31. Ibid.

32. Deposition of Solomon Cole, MA v. 154: 160.

33. Quoted in Frederick Freeman, *The History of Cape Cod: The Annals of Barnstable County including the District of Mashpee* (Boston, 1860), 1:514.

34. See Feer, *Shays's Rebellion*, 530–39.

35. Mount Washington Petition, MA v. 188: 80–81.

36. *Independent Chronicle* (Boston), August 21, 1783; Robert J. Taylor, *Western Massachusetts in the Revolution* (Providence: Brown University Press, 1954), 109.

37. Feer, *Shays's Rebellion*, 540.

38. Ibid., 115.

39. *Massachusetts Spy* (Worcester), April 18, 1782.

40. John L. Brooke, "To the Quiet of the People: Revolutionary Settlements and Civil Unrest in Western Massachusetts, 1774–1789," *William and Mary Quarterly*, 3rd ser., 46 (1989): 431–38.

41. Quotes from *Massachusetts Spy* (Worcester), May 29, 1782; the disturbances caused by Samuel Ely in the 1782 are described in Feer, *Shays's Rebellion*, 142–64; and Robert E. Moody, "Samuel Ely: Forerunner of Shays," *New England Quarterly* 5, no. 1 (1932): 105–34.

42. Feer, *Shays's Rebellion*, 143–44.

43. *Independent Chronicle* (Boston), May 23, 1782.

44. Feer, *Shays's Rebellion*, 146–47.

45. *Providence Gazette*, June 22, 1782.

46. Ibid; Feer, *Shays's Rebellion*, 147.

47. *Massachusetts Gazette* (Springfield), June 25, 1782.

48. "Terms of Agreement," Northampton, June 13, 1782, MA v. 236: 514.

49. Sheriff Porter to Governor Hancock June 14–15, 1782, MA v. 236: 517–18.

50. Sheriff Porter to Governor Hancock, June 18, 1782, MA v. 236: 160.

51. Feer, *Shays's Rebellion*, 153.

52. Moody, "Ely: Forerunner of Shays," 114.

53. Feer, *Shays's Rebellion*, 162–63.

54. Major Joseph Hawley to Ephraim Wright, April 16, 178[2], letter in "Shays's Rebellion," *American Historical Review* 36, no. 4 (1931): 776–78.

55. Moody, "Ely: Forerunner of Shays," 111.

56. Ibid., 112.

57. Ibid.

58. *Acts and Resolves of Massachusetts, 1782–83* (Boston, 1892), 6, https://archive.org/details/actsresolvespass178283mass.

59. Ibid., 10–24, 31–32; Taylor, *Western Massachusetts*, 117.

60. Roger Brown, *Redeeming the Republic*, 105.

61. *Acts and Resolves, 1782–83*, 238.

62. The Committee of the General Court Appointed to Repair to the County of Hampshire to Enquire into the Grounds of Dissatisfaction there, correct Misinformation and Remove Groundless Jealousies, MA v. 237: 377.

63. Roger Brown, *Redeeming the Republic*, 105.

64. Feer, *Shays's Rebellion*, 156; Taylor, *Western Massachusetts*, 119–20.

65. MA v. 237: 377–78.

66. Feer, *Shays Rebellion*, 170–71.

67. Ibid., 169–70.

68. Sheriff Caleb Hyde to Governor Hancock, October 2, 1782, MA v. 237: 455–56; Taylor, *Western Massachusetts*, 120.

69. *Acts and Resolves, 1782–83*, 105.

70. Richard H. Kohn, "The Inside History of the Newburgh Conspiracy: America and the Coup d'Etat," *William and Mary Quarterly*, 3rd ser., 27 (1970): 190.

71. *Journals of the Continental Congress, 1774–1789*, ed. Worthington C. Ford et al. (Washington, DC, 1904–37), 24:291.

72. Quoted in Kohn, "Newburgh Conspiracy," 189.

73. Don Higginbotham, *The War of American Independence: Military Attitudes, Policies, and Practice, 1763–1789* (New York: Macmillan, 1971), 408–12.

74. Woody Holton, *Unruly Americans and the Origins of the Constitution* (New York: Hill and Wang, 2007), 67–69.

75. Robert Szatmary, *Shays' Rebellion: The Making of an Agrarian Insurrection* (Amherst: University of Massachusetts Press, 1980), 30–36.

76. *Boston Gazette*, June 2, 1783.

77. Quoted in Feer, *Shays Rebellion*, 171.

78. Quoted in Roger Brown, *Redeeming the Republic*, 107.

79. "An Act for Apportioning and Assessing a Tax of Two Hundred Thousand Pounds," in *Early American Imprints, Series 1, Evans*, no. 19423.

80. Roger Brown, *Redeeming the Republic*, 247.

81. *Hampshire Herald* (Springfield), September 7, 1784, quoted in Brown, *Redeeming the Republic*, 107–8.

CHAPTER TWO: Governor Bowdoin Faces the Regulators

1. Van Beck Hall, *Politics Without Parties: Massachusetts, 1780–1791* (Pittsburgh: University of Pittsburgh Press, 1972), 136–38.

2. Gordon E. Kershaw, *James Bowdoin II: Patriot and Man of the Enlightenment* (Lanham, MD: University Press of America, 1991); William M. Fowler, *The Baron of Beacon Hill: A Biography of John Hancock* (Boston: Houghton Mifflin, 1980).

3. *Acts and Resolves of Massachusetts, 1784–85* (Boston, 1892), 707, https://archive .org/details/actsresolvespass178485mass.

4. Ibid., 708–9.

5. Ibid., 709.

6. Ibid., 186–92.

7. Roger H. Brown, *Redeeming the Republic: Federalists, Taxation, and the Origins of the Constitution* (Baltimore: Johns Hopkins University Press, 1993), 48–49.

8. Ibid., 17–21.

9. Edmund Cody Burnett, *The Continental Congress* (New York: Norton, 1964), 619–21.

10. Woody Holton, *Unruly Americans and the Origins of the Constitution* (New York: Hill and Wang, 2008), 65–82.

11. For conversion between pounds and dollars, see John J. McCusker, "How Much Is That in Real Money? A Historical Price Index for Use as a Deflator of Money Values in the Economy of the United States," *Proceedings of the American Antiquarian Society* 101, no. 2 (1991): 333, table A-3, http://www.americanantiquarian.org/proceedings/44517778.pdf.

12. *Acts and Resolves, 1784–85*, 725–33.

13. Ibid.

14. Ibid., 734–35.

15. Roger Brown, *Redeeming the Republic*, 14.

16. *Acts and Resolves, 1784–85*, 734–35.

17. Ibid., 821–22.

18. Robert A. Feer, *Shays's Rebellion* (New York: Garland, 1988), 541–43.

19. *Massachusetts Centinel*, February 8, 1786.

20. Ibid.

21. *Hampshire Herald*, March 7, 1786, reprinted in *Massachusetts Gazette* (Boston), April 3, 1786.

22. *Massachusetts Centinel*, March 1, 1786.

23. *Massachusetts Centinel*, February 11, 1786.

24. Robert Szatmary, *Shays' Rebellion: The Making of an Agrarian Insurrection* (Amherst: University of Massachusetts Press, 1980), 53.

25. Robert J. Taylor, *Western Massachusetts in the Revolution* (Providence: Brown University Press, 1954), 198.

26. *Acts and Revolves, 1784–85*, 580–605.

27. Ibid., 510–20.

28. Roger Brown, *Redeeming the Republic*, 109.

29. *Acts and Resolves of Massachusetts, 1786–87* (Boston, 1893), 313–14, https://archive.org/details/actsresolvespass178687mass.

30. See Holton, *Unruly Americans*, 72–73.

31. Ibid., 77.

32. Ibid., 131–34.

33. Hall, *Politics Without Parties*, 204.

34. *Independent Chronicle and the Universal Advertiser* (Boston), August 3, 1786.

35. *United States Chronicle* (Providence, RI), July 13, 1786.

36. *Independent Chronicle and the Universal Advertiser* (Boston), July 27, 1786.

37. *Worcester Magazine*, fourth week, August 1786, v. II, 251.

38. *Hampshire Herald*, September 19, 1786, quoted in Taylor, *Western Massachusetts*, 141–42.

39. *Independent Chronicle and the Universal Advertiser* (Boston), August 31, 1786.

40. Quoted in George Richards Minot, *History of the Insurrections in Massachusetts In the Year Seventeen-Hundred and Eighty Six and the Rebellion Consequent Thereon*, 2nd ed. (Boston: James W. Burditt, 1810), 34–36.

41. Ibid., 36.

42. Taylor, *Western Massachusetts*, 140.

43. Quoted in ibid., 143.

44. Ibid.

45. "The Bowdoin and Temple Papers (1783–1790)," in *Collections of the Massachusetts Historical Society*, 7th ser., VI (1907): 108–10.

46. *Independent Chronicle* (Boston), September 7, 1786.

47. Ibid.

48. Gov. Bowdoin to General Warmer, September 2, 1786, Massachusetts Archives (hereafter MA) v. 190: 228, Massachusetts State Archives, Boston.

49. Jonathan Warner to Governor Bowdoin, September 3, 1786, MA v. 190: 229.

50. Henshaw to Governor Bowdoin, September 7, 1786, MA v. 190: 237.

51. Feer, *Shays's Rebellion*, 196–97.

52. Ibid., 198–99.

53. *Boston Gazette*, September 11, 1786.

54. Loammi Baldwin to Governor Bowdoin, MA v. 190: 253–54.

55. Quoted in Robert A. Gross, "The Confidence Man and the Preacher: The Cultural Politics of Shays's Rebellion," in *In Debt to Shays: The Bicentennial of an Agrarian Rebellion*, ed. Robert A. Gross (Charlottesville: University Press of Virginia, 1993), 298.

56. MA v. 190: 250.

57. MA v. 190: 256.

58. MA v. 190: 258–59.

59. MA v. 190: 251.

60. Quoted in Feer, *Shays's Rebellion*, 199.

61. MA v. 190: 262.

62. David Cobb to Governor Bowdoin, September 13, 1786, in Shays' Rebellion Papers, 1786–87, Ms. N-923, microfilm P-152, Massachusetts Historical Society, Boston.

63. General John Patterson to Colonel Caleb Hyde, Lenox, September 10, 1786, MA v. 190: 241.

64. Sheriff Caleb Hyde to Governor Bowdoin, September 13, 1786, MA v. 190: 263–64.

65. Ibid.; also see *Hampshire Gazette* (Northampton), October 4, 1786.

66. Henry Van Schaack to Peter Van Schaack, September 18, 1786, quoted in Taylor, *Western Massachusetts*, 144–45.

67. Leonard L. Richards, *Shays's Rebellion: The American Revolution's Final Battle* (Philadelphia: University of Pennsylvania Press, 2002), 63–65.

CHAPTER THREE: Mobilizing Authority and Resistance

1. Robert A. Feer, *Shays's Rebellion* (New York: Garland, 1988), 361–62.

2. William Shepard to Governor Bowdoin, Massachusetts Archives (hereafter MA) v. 190: 266, Massachusetts State Archives, Boston.

3. Elisha Porter to Governor Bowdoin, September 25, 1786, MA v. 190: 265.

4. MA v. 190: 266.

5. William Shepard to Governor Bowdoin, September 29, 1786, MA v. 190: 291–92.

6. Ibid.

7. Leonard L. Richards, *Shays's Rebellion: The American Revolution's Final Battle* (Philadelphia: University of Pennsylvania Press, 2002), 5–7.

8. *Worcester Magazine*, second week, October 1786, v. II, 340.

9. David Sewell to Governor Bowdoin, MA v. 190: 294a–d.

10. Ibid.

11. Ibid.

12. MA v. 190: 290.

13. *Worcester Magazine*, second week, October 1786, v. II, 340.

14. MA v. 190: 294b.

15. Ibid.

16. MA v. 190: 291–92.

17. Richards, *Shays's Rebellion*, 46–48; Woody Holton, *Unruly Americans and the Origins of the Constitution* (New York: Hill and Wang, 2008), 94.

18. Joseph Parker Warren, "The Confederation and the Shays Rebellion," *American Historical Review* 11 no. 1 (1905): 49.

19. *Secret Journals of the Acts and Proceedings of Congress, From the First Meeting Thereof to the Dissolution of the Confederation, by the Adoption of the Constitution of the United States* (Boston, 1821), 1:269.

20. Sidney Kaplan, "Blacks in Massachusetts and the Shays' Rebellion," *Contributions in Black Studies* 8, article 2 (1986), http://scholarworks.umass.edu/cibs/vol8/iss1/2.

21. Quoted in Warren, "The Confederation and Shays Rebellion," 57.

22. Ibid.

23. Jere E. Daniell, *Experiment in Republicanism: New Hampshire Politics and the American Revolution, 1741–1794* (Cambridge, MA: Harvard University Press, 1970), 198; Alan Taylor, "Regulators and White Indians: Forms of Agrarian Resistance in Post-Revolutionary New England," in *In Debt to Shays: The Bicentennial of an Agrarian Rebellion*, ed. Robert A. Gross (Charlottesville: University Press of Virginia, 1993), 147–49.

24. *Acts and Resolves of Massachusetts, 1786–87* (Boston, 1893), 929, https://archive.org/details/actsresolvespass178687mass.

25. Ibid.

26. Ibid., 932.

27. *Worcester Magazine*, second week, October 1786, v. II, 334, 336.

28. Petition of the town of Dracut, September 29, 1786, Shays' Rebellion Collection, box 1, folder 2, American Antiquarian Society (hereafter AAS), Worcester, MA.

29. See Van Beck Hall, *Politics Without Parties: Massachusetts, 1780–1791* (Pittsburgh: University of Pittsburgh Press, 1972), 196.

30. Petition of the town of Dracut, September 29, 1786, AAS.

31. Petition of the town of Plympton, October 2, 1786, Shays' Rebellion Collection, box 1, folder 5, AAS.

32. Petition of the town of Groton, October 5, 1786, Shays' Rebellion Collection, box 1, folder 3, AAS.

33. Quoted in Feer, *Shays's Rebellion*, 237.

34. *Acts and Resolves, 1786–87*, 946.

35. Quoted in Feer, *Shays's Rebellion*, 240–41.

36. Ibid., 245.

37. *Acts and Resolves, 1786–87*, 90–97.

38. Ibid., 400.

39. Ibid., 117–30.

40. Ibid., 105–11.

41. Ibid., 113–16.

42. Ibid., 82.

43. Ibid., 87–90.

44. Ibid., 949–50; *Hampshire Gazette* (Springfield), November 15, 1786.

45. *Acts and Resolves, 1786–1787*, 102–3.

46. Ibid., 111–13.

47. Ibid., 159.

48. Ibid., 142–64.

CHAPTER FOUR:  Conflict from Springfield to Petersham

1. *Worcester Magazine*, fourth week, November 1786, v. II, 415; Robert A. Feer, *Shays's Rebellion* (New York: Garland, 1988), 317; *Hampshire Gazette* (Springfield), November, 29, 1786; George Richards Minot, *The History of the of the Insurrections in Massachusetts, in the year 1786, and the Rebellion Consequent Thereon*, 2nd ed. (Boston, 1810), 73.

2. Gary Shattuck, *Artful and Designing Men: The Trials of Job Shattuck and the Regulation of 1786–87* (Mustang, OK: Tate, 2013), 269.

3. Robert J. Taylor, *Western Massachusetts in the Revolution* (Providence: Brown University Press, 1954), 155; Minot, *History of the Insurrections*, 75–76.

4. General Jonathan Warner to Governor Bowdoin, Massachusetts Archives (hereafter MA) v. 189: 46–47, Massachusetts State Archives, Boston.

5. Oliver Prescott to Governor Bowdoin, MA v. 189: 41a.

6. Mary Cranch to Abigail Adams, quoted in Robert Szatmary, *Shays' Rebellion: The Making of an Agrarian Insurrection* (Amherst: University of Massachusetts Press, 1980), 92–93.

7. Shattuck, *Artful and Designing Men*, 290.

8. Leonard L. Richards, *Shays's Rebellion: The American Revolution's Final Battle* (Philadelphia: University of Pennsylvania Press, 2002), 20.

9. Quoted in Szatmary, *Shays' Rebellion*, 93.

10. John Noble, *A Few Notes on Shays Rebellion Reprinted from the Proceedings*

*of the American Antiquarian Society, October 21, 1902* (Worcester, MA, 1903), 15–16, https://archive.org/details/fewnotesonshaysroonobl.

11. Quoted in William Pencak, "'The Fine Theoretic Government of Massachusetts Is Prostrated to the Earth': The Response to Shays's Rebellion Reconsidered," in *In Debt to Shays: The Bicentennial of an Agrarian Rebellion,* ed. Robert A. Gross (Charlottesville: University Press of Virginia, 1993), 138–39.

12. MA v. 189: 146.

13. *Worcester Magazine,* first week, December 1786, v. II, 440.

14. Artemas Ward to Governor Bowdoin, December 7, 1786, in Shays' Rebellion Papers, Ms. N-923, microfilm P-152, Massachusetts Historical Society (hereafter MHS), Boston.

15. *Worcester Magazine,* second week, December 1786, v. II, 452.

16. Ibid.

17. *Worcester Magazine,* second week, December 1786, v. II, 453.

18. MA v.190: 297a.

19. MA v. 189: 429.

20. Quoted in Szatmary, *Shays' Rebellion,* 95.

21. Feer, *Shays's Rebellion,* 338.

22. "The Bowdoin and Temple Papers (1793–1790)," *Collections of the Massachusetts Historical Society,* 7th ser., VI (1907): 118.

23. Ibid., 119.

24. Ibid., 126.

25. Ibid.

26. Ibid., 121.

27. Ibid., 125.

28. Ibid.

29. Ibid.

30. Ibid., 122.

31. Ibid.

32. Feer, *Shays's Rebellion,* 346–47.

33. Ibid., 348–52.

34. Quoted in Taylor, *Western Massachusetts,* 159.

35. *American Herald* (Boston), January 15, 1787.

36. Ashburnham Town Petition, December 19, 1786, Shays' Rebellion Collection, box 1, folder 2, American Antiquarian Society (hereafter AAS), Worcester, MA.

37. New Braintree Town Petition, January 1, 1787, Shays' Rebellion Collection, box 1 folder 4, AAS.

38. Winchendon town petition, December 21, 1786, and January 13, 1787, Shays' Rebellion Collection, box 1, folder 7, AAS.

39. Ibid.

40. Brookfield petition, January 1, 1786, MA v. 190: 298; Brookfield petition, January 20, 1787, MA v. 190: 312–14.

41. *Hampshire Gazette* (Northampton), January 24, 1787.

42. *Collections of the Maine Historical Society*, II (1847): 250–54.

43. Ibid.

44. Governor Bowdoin to Rufus Putnam, January 17, 1787, MA v. 318: 65.

45. Rufus Putnam to Governor Bowdoin, Hadley, January 31, 1787, Shays' Rebellion Papers, Ms. N-923, microfilm P-152, MHS.

46. *Massachusetts Centinel*, January 17, 1787.

47. Sutton petition, January 17, 1787, MA v. 190: 305.

48. MA v. 190: 304.

49. MA v. 190: 304a; Van Beck Hall, *Politics Without Parties: Massachusetts, 1780–1791* (Pittsburgh: University of Pittsburgh Press, 1972), 225.

50. *Worcester Magazine*, fourth week, January 1787, v. II, 526.

51. "Type Script of General Lincoln's Order Book, 1787," Shays' Rebellion Collection, box 1, folder 13, AAS.

52. General William Shepard to Governor Bowdoin, January 19, 1787, MA v. 318: 74.

53. Szatmary, *Shays' Rebellion*, 100.

54. William Shepard to Governor Bowdoin, January 22, 1787, MA v. 318: 98.

55. William Shepard to Governor Bowdoin, January 24, 1787, MA v. 318: 110.

56. Quoted in Feer, *Shays's Rebellion*, 365.

57. *Worcester Magazine*, first week, February 1787, v. II, 535.

58. Quoted in Feer, *Shays's Rebellion*, 366.

59. Copy of letter from Luke Day to Daniel Shays, January 25, 1787, *Worcester Magazine*, second week, February 1787, v. II, 544.

60. Shepard to Bowdoin January 26, 1787, MA v. 190: 317.

61. Quoted in Feer, *Shays's Rebellion*, 367.

62. Richards, *Shays's Rebellion*, 29; Szatmary specifies that "fourteen or fifteen rounds of grapeshot" were fired; see Szatmary, *Shays' Rebellion*, 102.

63. General Shepard to Governor Bowdoin, January 26, 1787, MA v. 190: 317.

64. Ibid.

65. Richard D. Brown, "Shays's Rebellion and Its Aftermath: A View From Springfield, Massachusetts, 1787," *William and Mary Quarterly*, 3rd ser., 40 (1983): 606–7.

66. Ibid., 607.

67. Benjamin Lincoln to Governor Bowdoin, January 28, 1787, MA v. 190: 319.

68. *Worcester Magazine*, second week, February 1787, v. II, 552.

69. MA v. 190: 337.

70. *Worcester Magazine*, second week, February 1787, v. II, 552.

71. Feer, *Shays's Rebellion*, 373–74.

72. *Worcester Magazine*, second week, February 1787, v. II, 552.

73. Noble, "A Few Notes on Shays's Rebellion," 25.

74. Feer, *Shays's Rebellion*, 379.

75. Szatmary, *Shays' Rebellion*, 105.

CHAPTER FIVE: Governing the Regulators and Regulating Government

1. Quoted in Gregory H. Nobles, " 'Yet the Old Republicans Still Persevere': Samuel Adams, John Hancock, and the Crisis of Popular Leadership in Revolutionary Massachusetts, 1775–1790," in *The Transforming Hand of Revolution: Reconsidering the American Revolution as a Social Movement*, ed. Ronald Hoffman and Peter J. Albert (Charlottesville: University Press of Virginia, 1995), 280.

2. *Acts and Resolves of Massachusetts, 1786–87* (Boston, 1893), 425, https://archive.org/details/actsresolvespass178687mass.

3. Ibid., 425–26.

4. Ibid., 427; Robert A. Feer, *Shays's Rebellion* (New York: Garland, 1988), 384.

5. *Acts and Resolves, 1786–87*, 432.

6. Feer, *Shays's Rebellion*, 391.

7. Benjamin Lincoln to Governor Bowdoin, Pittsfield, February 17, 1787, Shays' Rebellion Papers, Ms. N-923, microfilm P-152, Massachusetts Historical Society (hereafter MHS), Boston.

8. "Type Script of General Lincoln's Order Book, 1787," Shays' Rebellion Collection, box 1, folder 13, 17, 18, American Antiquarian Society (hereafter AAS), Worcester, MA.

9. Ibid.

10. *Worcester Magazine*, third week, February 1787, v. II, 565.

11. Robert Szatmary, *Shays' Rebellion: The Making of an Agrarian Insurrection* (Amherst: University of Massachusetts Press, 1980), 108.

12. Ibid.

13. Feer, *Shays's Rebellion*, 402.

14. "The Bowdoin and Temple Papers (1783–1790)," *Collections of the Massachusetts Historical Society*, 7th ser., VI (1907): 153–54.

15. See Robert A. Gross, "The Confidence Man and the Preacher: The Cultural Politics of Shays's Rebellion," in *In Debt to Shays: The Bicentennial of an Agrarian Rebellion*, ed. Robert A. Gross (Charlottesville: University Press of Virginia, 1993), 301–2.

16. Royall Tyler to Benjamin Lincoln, Massachusetts Archives (hereafter MA) v. 318: 232, Massachusetts State Archives, Boston.

17. "Bowdoin and Temple Papers," 143.

18. Lincoln to Bowdoin, Pittsfield, February 27, Lincoln Papers, Ms. N-830, microfilm P-40, reel 8, MHS.

19. MA v. 190: 395.

20. Szatmary, *Shays' Rebellion*, 108–9.

21. Leonard L. Richards, *Shays's Rebellion: The American Revolution's Final Battle* (Philadelphia: University of Pennsylvania Press, 2002), 34.

22. *Connecticut Journal* (New Haven), February 28, 1787.

23. Royall Tyler to Benjamin Lincoln, MA v. 318: 232.

24. *New Haven Gazette*, February 15, 1787.

25. *Boston Gazette*, February 19, 1787.

26. *United States Chronicle* (Providence, RI), February 15, 1787.

27. *Hampshire Gazette*, March 14, 1787.

28. MA v. 190: 393–94.

29. *Acts and Resolves, 1786–87*, 425–26.

30. Ibid., 424.

31. MA v. 189: 143.

32. "The Bowdoin and Temple Papers," 141–42.

33. Hopkinton petition, February 1, 1787, Shays' Rebellion Collection, box 1, folder 3, AAS.

34. Paxton petition February 5, 1787, Shays' Rebellion Collection, box 1, folder 5, AAS.

35. Lunenberg petition February 19, 1787, Shays' Rebellion Collection, box 1, folder 4, AAS.

36. Shirley petition February 5, 1787, Shays' Rebellion Collection, box 1, folder 6, AAS.

37. *Acts and Resolves, 1786–87*, 176–80.

38. Ibid., 198–200.

39. Ibid., 516–17; Feer, *Shays's Rebellion*, 385–88.

40. Robert J. Taylor, *Western Massachusetts in the Revolution* (Providence: Brown University Press, 1954), 165.

41. Feer, *Shays's Rebellion*, 414.

42. Ibid., 395.

43. Quoted in Feer, *Shays's Rebellion*, 396–97.

44. Ibid.

45. Richard D. Brown, "Shays's Rebellion and Its Aftermath: The View from Springfield, Massachusetts, 1787," *William and Mary Quarterly*, 3rd ser., 40 (1983): 614.

46. Quoted in Feer, *Shays's Rebellion*, 409.

47. Stephen T. Riley, "Dr. Whiting and Shays's Rebellion," *American Antiquarian Society Proceedings* 66 (1957): 124.

48. MA v. 190: 417.

49. Riley, "Dr. Whiting," 130.

50. Van Beck Hall, *Politics Without Parties: Massachusetts, 1780–1791* (Pittsburgh: University of Pittsburgh Press, 1972), 236.

51. Szatmary, *Shays' Rebellion*, 111.

52. Ibid., 112–13.

53. Ibid., 13.

54. Richards, *Shays's Rebellion*, 56–58.

55. MA v. 189: 426.

56. *Massachusetts Gazette* (Boston), May 29, 1787.

57. MA v. 190: 16.

58. *Salem Mercury*, July 10, 1787.

59. MA v. 189: 409.

60. MA v. 189: 411–12.

61. MA v. 189: 414.

62. MA v. 189: 415.

63. Ibid.

64. Gregory H. Nobles, "The Politics of Patriarchy in Shays's Rebellion: The Case of Henry McCulloch," *Dublin Seminar for New England Folklife: Annual Proceedings* 10 (1985): 45.

65. "An Episode of Shays's Rebellion," *Magazine of History with Notes and Queries* 22, no. 3 (March 1916): 104–7.

66. Hall, *Politics Without Parties*, 253–54.

67. Feer, *Shays's Rebellion*, 449.

68. MA v. 30: 198–205.

69. *Worcester Magazine*, first week, July 1787, v. III, 180.

70. *Worcester Magazine*, fourth week, June 1787, v. III, 167.

71. MA v. 189: 329.

72. MA v. 189: 347.

73. *New Haven Chronicle*, June 26, 1787.

74. MA v. 190: 27.

75. Feer, *Shays's Rebellion*, 419.

76. George Richards Minot, *The History of the of the Insurrections in Massachusetts, in the year 1786, and the Rebellion Consequent Thereon*, 2nd. ed. (Boston, 1810), 189–91.

77. *Massachusetts Gazette* (Boston), March 14, 1788.

EPILOGUE: Shays's Rebellion and the Constitution

1. Samuel Eliot Morison and William Manning, "William Manning's The Key of Liberty," *William and Mary Quarterly*, 3rd ser., 13 (1956): 242–43.

2. "From Thomas Jefferson to Edward Carrington, 16 January 1787," Founders Online, National Archives (http://founders.archives.gov/documents/Jefferson /01-11-02-0047, ver. 2014-05-09), Source: *The Papers of Thomas Jefferson*, vol. 11, *1 January–6 August 1787*, ed. Julian P. Boyd (Princeton: Princeton University Press, 1955), 48–50.

3. "To James Madison from Thomas Jefferson, 30 January 1787," Founders Online, National Archives (http://founders.archives.gov/documents/Madison/01-09 -02-0126, ver. 2014-05-09), Source: *The Papers of James Madison*, vol. 9, *9 April 1786– 24 May 1787 and Supplement 1781–1784*, ed. Robert A. Rutland and William M. E. Rachal (Chicago: University of Chicago Press, 1975), 247–52.

4. "Thomas Jefferson to Abigail Adams, 22 February 1787," Founders Online, National Archives (http://founders.archives.gov/documents/Adams/04-07-02-0187, ver. 2014-05-09), Source: *The Adams Papers: Adams Family Correspondence*, vol. 7, *January 1786–February 1787*, ed. C. James Taylor, Margaret A. Hogan, Celeste Walker, Anne Decker Cecere, Gregg L. Lint, Hobson Woodward, and Mary T. Claffey (Cambridge, MA: Harvard University Press, 2005), 468–69.

5. See Robert A. East, "The Massachusetts Conservatives in the Critical Period," in *The Era of the American Revolution*, ed. Richard B. Morris (New York: Harper and Row, 1939), 371–75.

6. Van Beck Hall, *Politics Without Parties: Massachusetts, 1780–1791* (Pittsburgh: University of Pittsburgh Press, 1972), 260.

7. Leonard L. Richards, *Shays's Rebellion: The American Revolution's Final Battle* (Philadelphia: University of Pennsylvania Press, 2002), 124.

8. Quoted in East, "Massachusetts Conservatives," 377–78.

9. Richard Beeman, *Plain, Honest Men: The Making of the American Constitution* (New York: Random House, 2010), 113.

10. Hall, *Politics Without Parties*, 262.

11. East, "Massachusetts Conservatives," 379; also see Richards, *Shays's Rebellion*, 128.

12. "From George Washington to David Humphreys, 22 October 1786," Founders Online, National Archives (http://founders.archives.gov/documents/Washington /04-04-02-0272, ver. 2014-02-12), Source: *The Papers of George Washington, Confederation Series*, vol. 4, *2 April 1786–31 January 1787*, ed. W. W. Abbot (Charlottesville: University Press of Virginia, 1995), 296–97.

13. "To George Washington from Henry Knox, 23 October 1786," Founders Online, National Archives (http://founders.archives.gov/documents/Washington/04 -04-02-0274, ver. 2014-02-12).

14. "From George Washington to Henry Knox, 26 December 1786," Founders Online, National Archives (http://founders.archives.gov/documents/Washington/04 -04-02-0409, ver. 2014-02-12).

15. "From George Washington to James Madison, 5 November 1786," Founders Online, National Archives (http://founders.archives.gov/documents/Washington/04 -04-02-0299, ver. 2014-02-12).

16. "From George Washington to Lafayette, 25 March 1787," Founders Online, National Archives (http://founders.archives.gov/documents/Washington/04-05-02 -0103, ver. 2014-02-12).

17. Robert Szatmary, *Shays' Rebellion: The Making of an Agrarian Insurrection* (Amherst: University of Massachusetts Press, 1980), 123.

18. Woody Holton, *Unruly Americans and the Origins of the Constitution* (New York: Hill and Wang, 2008), 218; Beeman, *Plain, Honest Men*, 290–91. Massachusetts delegate Elbridge Gerry was opposed to allowing the federal forces to enter a state to put down an internal matter. During the convention, Gerry argued, "More blood would have been spilled" during the rebellion if federal troops "had intermeddled." Max Farrand, ed., *The Records of the Federal Convention of 1787*, 3 vols. (New Haven: Yale University Press, 1911), 2:317.

19. Holton, *Unruly Americans*, 182.

20. Samuel Bannister Harding, *The Contest over the Ratification of the Federal Constitution in the State of Massachusetts* (New York: Longmans, Green, 1896), 50.

21. Richard D. Brown, "Shays's Rebellion and the Ratification of the Federal

Constitution in Massachusetts," in *Beyond Confederation: Origins of the Constitution and American National Identity*, ed. Richard Beeman, Stephen Botein, and Edward C. Carter II (Chapel Hill: University of North Carolina Press, 1987), 113–27.

22. Richards, *Shays's Rebellion*, 145–46.

23. Ibid., 144.

24. Ibid., 144–47; Szatmary, *Shays' Rebellion*, 133.

25. *Debates and Proceedings in the Convention of the Commonwealth of Massachusetts Held in the Year 1788* (Boston: William White, 1856), 404–5.

26. Hall, *Politics Without Parties*, 181, 225.

27. Quoted in Pauline Maier, *Ratification: The People Debate the Constitution, 1787–1788* (New York: Simon and Shuster, 2011), 187–88.

28. Ibid., 187–88; Merrill Jensen, John P. Kaminski et al., eds., *The Documentary History of the Ratification of the Constitution* (Madison: Wisconsin Historical Society Press, 1976–), vol. VI: 1346, http://www.wisconsinhistory.org/ratification/.

29. Maier, *Ratification*, 207–8.

30. Ibid., 211.

# Suggested Further Reading

While every general history and textbook that covers early American history provides at least some coverage of the events that come to be called Shays's Rebellion, there have also been book-length works on the topic. The first was written within two years of the conflict by George Richards Minot, a Harvard-educated lawyer and clerk of the Massachusetts House of Representatives. Minot's *The History of the of the Insurrections in Massachusetts, in the year 1786, and the Rebellion Consequent Thereon*, 2nd ed. (Boston, 1810), was primarily an attempt to defend the actions of government, but he also tried to provide some understanding of the people he called insurgents. Minot's narrative provides readers with a good idea of the sentiments of government supporters, and it also includes excerpts from some of the petitions of the conventions and regulators. The best and most thorough exploration of the historiography of Shays's Rebellion from Minot to the 1990s is Robert A. Gross's "White Hats and Hemlocks: Daniel Shays and the Legacy of the Revolution," in *The Transforming Hand of Revolution: Reconsidering the American Revolution as a Social Movement*, ed. Ronald Hoffman and Peter J. Albert (Charlottesville: University Press of Virginia, 1995), 286–345.

In the modern era, several professional historians have provided different perspectives on the causes and consequences of the conflict in book-length explorations. Robert A. Feer's dissertation ("Shays's Rebellion," Ph.D. dissertation, Harvard University, 1955, published by Garland Press in 1988) remains essential because of its use of a wide variety of primary sources and its compilation of town and county petitions from 1782 to 1787. Robert Szatmary's monograph, *Shays' Rebellion: The Making of an Agrarian Insurrection* (Amherst: University of Massachusetts Press, 1980), argues that the insurgents were motivated primarily by private debt, which was triggered by a transatlantic credit contraction in the mid-1780s. In Szatmary's view, indebted farmers—who had been accustomed to face-to-face financial transactions with neighbors—became indebted after the war and turned against merchants and their allies in government who sought to seize their property when they could not pay their debts.

By contrast, Leonard L. Richards's *Shays's Rebellion: The American Revolution's Final Battle* (Philadelphia: University of Pennsylvania Press, 2002) shows that, while debt cases increased following the revolution, they peaked in most counties about a year or two before the court closures that began in the summer of 1786. In addition, many of the men who closed the courts were not debtors but were in fact creditors in their own right. For Richards, a more compelling explanation was the anger directed at the holders of state debt—the wealthy merchants and government officials who had purchased soldier's notes and other government securities and were advocating heavy taxation in order to secure windfall profits. Richards shows exactly how much government debt some men held, and his work is also valuable because it traces some of the local networks of rank-and-file regulators by linking those men who took the oaths of allegiance with local records and town histories.

Other significant interpretations come in article-length works or from historians who make Shays's Rebellion an important part of broader historical interpretations. Older interpretations include J. R. Pole, *Political Representation in England and the Origins of the American Republic* (New York: St. Martin's, 1966), which shows that the 1780 Massachusetts Constitution solidified a legislative balance of power that favored the more populous, wealthy, and commercially oriented eastern third of the state and provided supporters of deflationary fiscal policy and high taxes with the ability to put their policies into practice. For an interpretation that emphasizes high taxes and the weakness of the state and the federal government to respond early and decisively to the crisis, see Forrest McDonald, *E Pluribus Unum: The Formation of the American Republic, 1776–1790* (Boston: Houghton Mifflin, 1965), and for an early argument that stresses the role of debt and the importance of seeing the conflict in Massachusetts as one example of a broader pattern of agrarian discontent, see Barbara Karsky, "Agrarian Radicalism in the Late Revolutionary Period (1780–1795)," in *New Wine in Old Skins: A Comparative View of Socio-political Structures and Values Affecting the American Revolution*, ed. Erich Angermann, Marie-Luise Frings, and Hermann Wellenreuther (Stuttgart: Klett, 1976), 87–114.

More recently, one essential work is Roger H. Brown's *Redeeming the Republic: Federalists, Taxation, and the Origins of the Constitution* (Baltimore: Johns Hopkins University Press, 1993). Brown shows that the federal government's inability to raise revenue directly during the Confederation era was a fundamental factor in sparking and shaping the Constitutional Convention. In studies of several states, including Massachusetts, Brown shows that every state tried through taxation to provide the funds requested by Congress, but none was successful. Brown shows that Massachusetts's efforts to raise taxes were the most strenuous, and the state legislature's decision to attempt to meet the federal requisition of 1785 through rigorous enforcement of tax collection was an important trigger of the conflict. Woody Holton's *Unruly Americans and the Origins of the Constitution* (New York: Hill and Wang, 2008) combines Brown's emphasis on taxation with Richards's focus on creditors to argue that taxes in Massachusetts were so high because creditors were so firmly in charge. In other states, legislatures either made choices between supporting state or federal creditors or were controlled or influenced by more popular forces that advocated relief measures like paper money or tender laws. In Massachusetts, however, the legislature decided to levy a tax that would support both state creditors and the federal requisition.

While Holton and Richards both emphasize the importance that individual financial incentives played for elite public creditors in Massachusetts, Richard Buel Jr. argues that one must also pay attention to the larger ideology of public creditors and their supporters, which emphasized the need of the state to make short-term sacrifices (what today would be called programs of "austerity"), in order to buttress both the creditworthiness and the stature of the fledgling states and the republic as a whole. Buel's article, entitled "The Public Creditor Interest in Massachusetts Politics, 1780–86," is just one of many essential works found in the collection edited by Robert A. Gross and entitled *In Debt to Shays: The Bicentennial of an Agrarian Rebellion* (Charlottesville: University Press of Virginia, 1993). This wide-ranging collection covers issues related to debt and financial questions, the role that religion and community played in shaping the resistance to government, and different interpretations of the response taken by government. While most interpretations since George Minot have argued that the state government overreacted in dealing with the regulators, William Pencak's contribution to *In Debt to Shays*, entitled " 'The Fine Theoretic Government of Massachusetts Is Prostrated to the Earth': The Response to Shays's Rebellion Reconsidered," is an effort to rehabilitate the government response by arguing that the rebellion was more radical and potentially disruptive than most have suggested and that the government showed a great deal of restraint.

Most recent works that discuss the rebellion, however, would disagree with Pencak and in fact would argue that calling the conflict "Shays's Rebellion" is to take the supporters of government's interpretation as a starting point. Historians like Robert A. Gross, Alan Taylor, Gregory Nobles, and Ronald Formisano argue that the people who protested against the Massachusetts government in 1786 and 1787 called themselves "regulators" and that is how they should be seen. The term *regulator* was first used by the English in the seventeenth century to describe protest efforts that aimed to curb abuses of government power, and before the American Revolution two distinct protest movements—one in South Carolina and the other in North Carolina—called themselves "regulators." Formisano was among the first to make this point in an article entitled "Teaching Shays / The Regulation: Historiographical Problems as Tools for Learning," *Uncommon Sense: A Newsletter of the Omohundro Institute for Early American History and Culture* 106 (Winter 1998): 24–35. Formisano also makes this argument in his *For the People: American Populist Movements from the Revolution to the 1850s* (Chapel Hill: University of North Carolina Press, 2008). Also see Alan Taylor's "Regulators and White Indians: Forms of Agrarian Resistance in Post-Revolutionary New England," in *In Debt to Shays*; Gregory Nobles, " 'Satan, Smith, Shattuck, and Shays': The People's Leaders in the Massachusetts Regulation," in *Revolutionary Founders: Rebels, Radicals, and Reformers in the Making of the Nation*, ed. Alfred F. Young, Gary B. Nash, and Ray Raphael (New York: Alfred A. Knopf, 2011), 215–32; and Robert A. Gross, "A Yankee Rebellion? The Regulators, New England, and the New Nation," *New England Quarterly* 82 (2009): 112–35.

Other works place the rebellion (or the regulation) in regional or local contexts. The first work to do so was Robert J. Taylor, *Western Massachusetts in the Revolution* (Providence: Brown University Press, 1954). Taylor's work covers the period from the late colonial period through the ratification of the Constitution. A much more complex and fine-grained examination can be found in the work of John L. Brooke, especially his monograph *The Heart of the Commonwealth: Society and Political Culture in Worcester County, Massachusetts, 1713–1861* (Cambridge: Cambridge University Press, 1990), which provides a deep study of the social, cultural, and political change in Worcester County, while his "To the Quiet of the People: Revolutionary Settlements and Civil Unrest in Western Massachusetts, 1774–1789," *William and Mary Quarterly*, 3rd ser., 46, no. 3 (1989): 425–62, compares and contrasts the nature of protest in Worcester, Hampshire, and Berkshire counties. Among other insights, Brooke's careful research shows that debt relations did shape the crisis but not in the straightforward way suggested by Szatmary. Meanwhile, Christopher Clark's *The Roots of Rural Capitalism: Western Massachusetts, 1780–1860* (Ithaca, NY: Cornell University Press, 1990), which focuses on the Connecticut River valley, supports Szatmary's view that a cultural conflict existed between farming communities where economic exchange was embedded in more complex social interactions and more long-distance and impersonal exchanges that were strictly economic in nature. A relatively neglected area of examination is Middlesex County, and a new work by Gary Shattuck, *Artful and Designing Men: The Trials of Job Shattuck and the Regulation of 1786–87* (Mustang, OK: Tate, 2013), provides a wealth of detail on the town of Groton and the complex relationships between Job Shattuck and others in town and beyond.

The primary sources related to Shays's Rebellion are plentiful, but nearly all of the personal accounts are from the perspective of government officials. While many of the primary sources used in this study can be viewed only by those with the ability to travel to archives, there is a very useful website created by Springfield Technical Community College, "Shays Rebellion and the Making of a Nation" (http://shays rebellion.stcc.edu/), which includes narratives, character sketches, and transcripts of primary sources. While most Massachusetts newspapers were centered in Boston, and essentially all of them were critical of the regulators and the convention movement, they do provide eyewitness accounts of court actions and armed conflict, and they also print some documents from the regulators themselves. Many academic libraries, as well as some public libraries, subscribe to the electronic versions of Early American Newspapers made available by Readex (http://www.readex.com/content /early-american-newspapers-1690-1922-series). Scanning and digitization have made many sources available, but unfortunately most primary sources related to Shays's Rebellion are still only accessible in archives. The most important collections are the Massachusetts State Archives in Boston, which has several volumes (which were organized in the nineteenth century and microfilmed in the twentieth) that deal explicitly with the rebellion, with volumes 189 and 190 being the most useful for this study. These volumes include correspondence between militia leaders, sheriffs, and government officials, as well as town petitions and a few documents written by the regulators. Other volumes that dealt with town petitions, as well as depositions and other court documents, were also consulted. The state archives also hold records of state government, including the session laws and resolves, and it has a webpage that conveniently links to electronic copies of the published laws (http://www.mass .gov/anf/research-and-tech/oversight-agencies/lib/massachusetts-acts-and-resolves -1692-to-1959.html). The Massachusetts Historical Society had microfilm and manuscript papers of several prominent government figures in the rebellion, including Robert Treat Paine, Benjamin Lincoln, Henry Knox, Elisha Porter, and Theodore Sedgwick. It also has a microfilm collection of miscellaneous letters called the Shays' Rebellion Papers, manuscript P-152. The American Antiquarian Society has a Shays' Rebellion Collection, including a list of petitions from towns in 1786 and 1787, and some of the depositions collected by Robert Treat Paine as he worked to build criminal cases against suspected insurgents in the spring of 1787.

The other electronic sources that can be helpful for locating primary sources are digitized copies of town histories and historical society collections that have entered the public domain. The Bowdoin and Temple Papers, published as part of the *Collections of the Massachusetts Historical Society*, 7th ser., VI (1907), has correspondence of Governor Bowdoin dated between September 1786 and the spring of 1787. Also, the *Collections of the Maine Historical Society*, vol. II (Portland, ME, 1847), includes a copy of a letter by Rufus Putnam describing his conversation with Daniel Shays. The Library of Congress has made the *Letters of Delegates to Congress, 1774–1789*, available online at http://memory.loc.gov/ammem/amlaw/lwdg.html. These letters are helpful in understanding how some prominent American political figures were understanding the conflict in Massachusetts as it unfolded. In addition, the National Archives project to put the papers of several founding fathers online can be found at http:// founders.archives.gov. This site was useful for examining George Washington's correspondence related to Shays's Rebellion. Finally, the Wisconsin Historical Society Press had made available many of the volumes in its wide-ranging Documentary History of the Ratification of the Constitution Series available online, including all four volumes covering the Massachusetts Ratifying Convention at http://www.wis consinhistory.org/ratification/index.asp. A significant percentage of Massachusetts towns had town histories written in the nineteenth century by amateur gentleman historians who often had access to primary documents that are no longer extant or easily accessible. Of most use were C. O. Parmenter's *History of Pelham, Mass. from 1748 to 1898* (Amherst, MA, 1898), and Carpenter and Morehouse, comp., *The History of the Town of Amherst*, 2 vols. (Amherst, MA, 1896).

There is a very rich and deep literature of the Massachusetts colony's mobilization against the British. Richard Brown's *Revolutionary Politics in Massachusetts: The Boston Committee of Correspondence and the Towns* (Cambridge, MA: Harvard University Press, 1970) still provides an excellent way to see the networks of communication and mobilization that allowed colonial protest to build into a revolutionary movement. Ray Raphael, in *The First American Revolution: Before Lexington and Concord* (New York: New Press, 2002), provides a compelling and well-researched narrative of mobilization "from the bottom up" in the town of Worcester. L. Kinvin Wroth's introduction to a collection of primary sources that were copied on microfiche for the bicentennial celebration in 1976, *Province in Rebellion: A Documentary*

*History of the Founding of the Commonwealth of Massachusetts, 1774–75* (Cambridge, MA: Harvard University Press, 1975), provides a detailed chronology of events from the British response to the Tea Party through the battles of Lexington and Concord. T. H. Breen's recent *American Insurgents, American Patriots: The Revolution of the People* (New York: Hill and Wang, 2010) skillfully recovers a variety of specific examples that show the process of how "ordinary" colonists came to see armed resistance and violence against authority as a legitimate act.

Approachable introductions to the Revolutionary War itself can be found in Edward Countryman, *The American Revolution*, rev. ed. (New York: Hill and Wang, 2003), and Robert Middlekauff, *The Glorious Cause: The American Revolution, 1763–1789*, rev. ed. (New York: Oxford University Press, 2005). Middlekauff provides a traditional narrative approach focusing on the military, while Countryman focuses more on the cultural and political shifts and conflicts that shaped and were shaped by the war. The challenges of supplying the army are explored in E. Wayne Carp, *To Starve the Army at Pleasure: Continental Army Administration and American Popular Culture, 1775–1783* (Chapel Hill: University of North Carolina Press, 1984). The best explanation of the challenges of financing the war remains E. James Ferguson, *The Power of the Purse: A History of American Public Finance, 1776–1790* (Chapel Hill: University of North Carolina Press, 1961). The challenges facing Americans who wished to engage in Atlantic trade during the revolution is examined in Richard Buel Jr.'s *In Irons: Britain's Naval Supremacy and the American Revolutionary Economy* (New Haven: Yale University Press, 1998), while Barbara Clark Smith's *The Freedoms We Lost: Consent and Resistance in Revolutionary America* (New York: New Press, 2010) charts the rise and fall of crowd action and committee power in regulating economic exchange. The impact of the war on a local community is examined in Robert A. Gross's beautifully written community study *The Minutemen and Their World*, 25th anniversary ed. (New York: Hill and Wang, 2001).

The struggle to frame and ratify a state constitution is examined in two fine primary source collections. Oscar Handlin and Mary F. Handlin, eds., *The Popular Sources of Political Authority: Documents on the Massachusetts Constitution of 1780* (Cambridge, MA: Belknap Press of Harvard University Press, 1966), emphasizes the town returns to the 1780 Constitution, while Robert J. Taylor's *Massachusetts, Colony to Commonwealth: Documents on the Formation of the Constitution, 1775–1780* (Chapel Hill: University of North Carolina Press, 1961) has more coverage of the Berkshire Constitutionalists and other views from Western Massachusetts. Stephen E. Patterson's *Political Parties in Revolutionary Massachusetts* (Madison: University of Wisconsin Press, 1973) traces how different economic and cultural orientations led to conflict between eastern and western Massachusetts in the 1770s, while Van Beck Hall's *Politics Without Parties: Massachusetts, 1780–1791* (Pittsburgh: University of Pittsburgh Press, 1972) provides extensive analysis of the roll-call votes of the Massachusetts legislature in the 1780s, and he also provides additional help in understanding how the actions and decisions of the legislature shaped and were shaped by the regulators. Helpful in understanding the political partisanship between Samuel

Adams and John Hancock, as well as some insight into Hancock's appeal among non-elite westerners, is Gregory H. Nobles's "'Yet the Old Republicans Still Persevere': Samuel Adams, John Hancock, and the Crisis of Popular Leadership in Revolutionary Massachusetts, 1775–1790," in *Transforming Hand of Revolution*, 258–85. Joseph Parker Warren, "The Confederation and the Shays Rebellion," *American Historical Review* 11, no. 1 (1905): 42–67, is still useful in understanding the role of Henry Knox in trying to raise federal troops for the Springfield Armory.

Like the literature on the coming of the American Revolution, the literature on the Constitutional Convention and the ratification process is enormous. A readable and balanced introduction to the Constitutional Convention is Richard Beeman's *Plain Honest Men: The Making of the American Constitution* (New York: Random House, 2010), while an excellent introduction to the ratification debates can be found in Pauline Maier's *Ratification: The People Debate the Constitution, 1787–1788* (New York: Simon and Schuster, 2011). The impact of Shays's Rebellion on the ratification process is covered in the books by Szatmary, Richards, and Holton. While most historians emphasize that Shays's Rebellion impacted the Constitution, Richard Feer argues that the conflict played little role in stimulating the convention or shaping the document. See Feer, "Shays's Rebellion and the Constitution: A Study in Causation," *New England Quarterly* 42, no. 3 (1969): 388–410. While most historians have emphasized that Shays's Rebellion energized many to support a stronger central government, thus helping the Federalists, Richard D. Brown makes a persuasive argument that the Massachusetts state government's response to the uprising also generated more Anti-federalist sentiment at the ratifying convention. See Brown, "Shays's Rebellion and the Ratification of the Federal Constitution in Massachusetts," in *Beyond Confederation: Origins of the Constitution and American National Identity*, ed. Richard Beeman, Stephen Botein, and Edward C. Carter II (Chapel Hill: University of North Carolina Press, 1987), 113–27. Also see Brown's "Shays's Rebellion and Its Aftermath: The View From Springfield, Massachusetts, 1787," *William and Mary Quarterly*, 3rd ser., 40 (1983): 598–615.

# Index

Made in United States
North Haven, CT
06 August 2023